THE READER ORGANISATION

NEWS AND EVENTS

CALDERSTONES MANSION HOUSE

Liverpool City Council have awarded The Reader Organisation 'preferred bidder status' for Calderstones Mansion House in Calderstones Park, Liverpool. We will transform the Mansion House, Coach House and Stable Yard into an International Centre for Reading and Wellbeing, working with three local partners, Mersey Care NHS Trust, Plus Dane Group and University of Liverpool's CRILS (Centre for Research into Reading, Information and Linguistic Systems). The proposal includes establishing an international hub of shared reading practice and research; creating employment, personal development and volunteering opportunities; providing facilities for conferences and events. We expect to take up residency at Calderstones in August, whilst retaining our current base in West Everton; full development will be phased and expected to complete in December 2015. Read more in Jane Davis's regular piece on p.95

APPRENTICESHIP FUNDRAISING SUCCESS

Since April last year, we have been fundraising for our Apprentice Scheme: Building Opportunities for Life, aiming to raise £14,000 to employ a young care leaver as a Reader Apprentice, providing them with the opportunity to build an independent and fulfilled life. The past few months have seen Reader staff and volunteers conquer the Three Peaks Challenge, run 5k dressed as Father Christmas in Liverpool's Santa Dash, recite Poetry by Heart and much more.

We are delighted to announce that, as of January 2013, the grand total raised stood at £17,664.75. Everyone at The Reader Organisation would like to say a huge thank you to those who donated their time and money to support this life-changing cause; because of you, we now have a new apprentice in our Wirral team, Zoe Jermy, who is already working to make a difference to her local community and planning for her future.

SE100 INDEX

In recognition of our growth and positive social impact, The Reader Organisation has been included in the 2012 RBS Social Enterprise 100 Index. We grew by 23% in 2012, placing us at #70 in the top 100 UK social businesses and confirming our place as a key player in this dynamic sector.

CONTENTS

OUR LIVERPOOL HOME?
© Roisin Hyland

See p. 95

IT DOES YOUR HEAD IN

Philip Davis

N euroscience makes you friends and enemies. I am no expert in this area (neuroscience; I know about friends and enemies). I barely understand my hippocampus from my elbow. A colleague gave me a 3D model of the brain the other day, to disassemble, play with and then reconnect. I could do the first and the second but then couldn't get the pieces back together again. They lay there, a nervous breakdown suffered by Humpty Dumpty.

But I have recently recommenced work in this area – reading serious literature and brain-imaging – with the help of experts at the University of Liverpool, Rhiannon Corcoran and Noreen O'Sullivan. I tell them what I am interested in, they tell me their own interests and then what we need to do by way of experimental specimens in order to test a joint hypothesis. Later in the light of the first results, they kindly but sternly tell me what I may and (most often) may not conclude.

I love it – long before ever we slide the participants into the fMRI scanner, I relish the preliminary speculative conversations about what may go on in the movements and interconnections of the mind. It is like having a new language for momentarily separating out the many different underlying and interconnecting things we are able to do in thinking, without our usually (so to speak) having to think about it. Yet sometimes when you are reading poetry in particular you can almost feel those underlying motions that accompany the semantic content. Because it seems almost physical, it makes you think of the brain beneath mind, its firings, its sudden connectivities, somehow making for thought.

I am interested in the way that in immersed reading you journey along the lines, not quite knowing in advance where you are going, in the search for meaning. One of our eventual experimental specimens compared the following by the great Welsh seventeenth-century religious poet Henry Vaughan

O you did mourn to see me lost,
And all your care and counsels crossed:
Your anger I could kiss, and will:
But O! your grief, your grief does kill.

with our more prosaic modern version, to test the difference in brain response:

When I have hurt you I feel very bad,
Yet I can deal with your anger
Because of what I have done to you.
But your forgiveness is worse than anger.

It is not that the latter has no effect: words such as forgiveness and anger in this context still trigger feelings. But its flatness has nothing like the intensity of effect in relation to the extra dimensions of meaning added by powerful affect and autobiographical triggering. This is more than just a matter of 'style'. The literary examples create more intensity in the hippocampus (site of memory connected with emotion), and a greater activation of right-sided areas homologous to left-sided language-areas (such as the fusiform gyrus which scans for verbal meaning in ways similar to its scanning for facial recognition). I don't feel this is reductive or mechanised as the critics and enemies say it is: I feel as if I am seeing the brain come alive, and come alive more like a whole thing, informing the sudden excited realisation of meaning.

In the weeks and months that follow, whilst we apply for grants and make further technical developments, what we shall be looking for are two processes. One is to do with reappraisal capabilities – the ability of a reader to turn back in the midst of poetic time and instead of going on straightforwardly with the meaning, as in our prosaic examples, think again in the thick of the venture. Think of the mental turn-around required in 'Your anger I could kiss, and will: / But O! your grief, your grief does kill'. This shifts settled mental pathways.

The other is to do with what the friends in psychology call 'mentalisation': the ability to see oneself as if one was looking at another; related to the ability also to see others as though they were oneself. This higher level of self-reflection – like writers looking down at the poem in front of their eyes, like readers seeing themselves in the book, the book in themselves – creates a sort of second self sheerly by dint of being able to think about the self you are. That second self is neither entirely the same as the first one nor wholly detached from it either. It is a great evolutionary leap, crucial to the ability to think our own thoughts, to have our own experience: we shall look for its activation in the orbitofrontal cortex and allied areas.

And just as soon as I open my mouth about any of this, the press are on it as a sexy defence of 'the classics', radio want sixty-second bytes or bites at unearthly hours of day or night, and I find myself the object of overhyped praise or (worse) undeserved blame. One interviewer even asked me to find out what it was that was stimulated by *Fifty Shades of Grey*. As we say in Liverpool, it does your head in.

EDITOR'S PICKS

In this issue: fine new poetry from **David Constantine**, **Matthew Howard**, **Michael O'Neill** and **Ellen Storm**. In Poet on His Work **John Burnside** writes earnestly of the matters behind his poem 'From the Chinese'. We have striking new fiction from **John Kinsella** and **Greg Forshaw**.

In the first of a series on the RISE experience (Reading in a Secure Environment), **Jackie Kay** talks about reading to the women at HMP Styal, and her work is represented in both poetry and prose. There are arresting images of readers on the NYC subway by street photographer **Ourit Ben-Haim**, and publisher **David Fickling** is interviewed by Angela Macmillan.

FACE TO FACE

MEET THE POET

DAVID
CONSTANTINE
on p.26

Past, present and future?
I suppose that's how time works.
But our living apprehension of
time is always present. We feel
longing for a happier past or a
happier future *now*. This is very
obvious in the reading of poetry
which, however it moves, really
only has one tense: the present.

Past, present and future can't be
separated. So I find the compound
tenses very poignant, this famous
line in the conditional perfect, for
example: 'There would have been
a time for such a word.' The regret
in it is present.

**Which poet would you like to
have met?**
Ted Hughes. His work drew me
fully towards poetry (and then to
trying to write). It is through his
poetry that I have been brought
back closer to the natural world
and it's a major reason why I
work for a conservation organisation today. His work is not just
concerned with green nature; it's
broader and deeper than that.
I think I'm quoting Heaney's
description of him as 'a custodian
of the language and the land.'

MATTHEW
HOWARD
on p.41

10

Favourite place in the world
Because traps and falling into
them have a fascination for me,
I'll say Venice – the sky reaching
down to the water, bells tolling,
reflections. A motor-boat swerves
out of nowhere. The city is
sinking and never sinks; even in
front of you it's a memory. You
chug across the lagoon towards
Torcello: the Last Judgement
catches up with visitors at the
back; in the apse the Byzantine
Madonna, having seen infinite
glory or sadness or both, looks
past you into eternity.

MICHAEL
O'NEILL
on p.62

ELLEN
STORM
on p.88

**Do you prefer your poems to be
read silently or out loud?**
I don't mind how people read my
poems, as long as what they do
works for them. What I'm trying
to say is important – concepts
transmit in silence – but the
music is also important. Poems
become physical things through
sound and vibration and this is
what carries the emotion and
brings them alive. I tend to write
poems silently then read them
back aloud to hear how they
sound and feel in the mouth – the
shape of them.

JOHN BURNSIDE

© Helmut Fricke

THE POET ON HIS WORK

ON 'FROM THE CHINESE'

John Burnside

Usually, when I am writing the poem that will eventually close a book, I am not aware that this will be its role, but I knew that 'From the Chinese' would be the last poem in *Black Cat Bone* from the moment it started to form in my mind. As to the circumstances, the poem is quite literal: I suffer from sciatica and the best way to ease the pain and stiffness is to get my boots on and walk as far as I can. On this particular day, I didn't actually go very far, just to the end of the country road that runs past my house and up to the ridge of Fife; it was New Year's Eve, and the poem simply records the facts of a winter's day: crows, sheep foraging in my one good neighbour's field, that smell of frosted ditches, the straggling bones of winter gorse. The landscape here probably comes over as bleak and chill, which it is, but it is also very beautiful, in an austere way, and it is home to the animals and birds mentioned in the poem – and to many others. It is also my home ground. What isn't stated in the piece, however, is the fact that this landscape is threatened by a slew of opportunistic wind turbine developments – two of them directly adjacent to the nearby nature reserve at Gillingshill, all of them a direct threat to the waves of pink-footed geese who overwinter here (the only landowner on this ridge who isn't planning to cash in is, in fact, that one good neighbour whose sheep are mentioned in the poem). That this particular environmental threat is not stated is, of course, essential to the making of the piece: what comes across, hopefully, is the mood of the speaker, (who is both me, and not-me, an Everyman persona, one might say) who sees this local danger as indicative of a far bigger picture, in which the land, birds, all living creatures, not to mention his own well-being are irrelevant when set against the possible profits of the subsidy-harvesting classes.

The title is a little tongue-in-cheek. It refers to that tradition of Chinese poetry where the poet complains about some minor physical ailment – piles, say, or chilblains – then moves on to a stoical, or even celebratory response to the wider world. In my case, I wanted to celebrate the threatened life of this particular piece of terrain: the hare in flight, the buzzards and geese, who are seen as 'the old gods' of the land, (of course, hares and geese have both been sacred to my predecessors in this corner of Europe, and there is a certain poignancy in evoking those old ways in a climate where nothing is sacred but money). Of course, there is always a problem, with 'environmentalist' or 'eco' poetry of sliding into polemic, or the kind of editorialising you get at the end of certain TV nature programmes and thus diminishing the poem as *poem*. On the other hand, one wants to convey a certain mood, whether of elegy for what is about to be lost, or celebration of what continues in spite of the best efforts of bankers, developers and big landowners. I think, to make the environmentalist point, the poet has to work tangentially and create a mood which suggests, rather than argues – and this may be the limitation of art as a political weapon, that one tends to think of how well or badly the poem works as a poem first and foremost. I have been talking about the wind turbine issues for some years now, but I still constantly meet people who think they are 'a Good Thing', or a source of 'clean, green energy' (and there is subsidy money for artists, too, in backing this lie). It's heartbreaking, and it may well be the Silent Spring issue of our time, but poetry is unlikely to make a difference. What matters more is what public or literary figures are prepared to say on the issue: I applaud Frieda Hughes' stand on this, for example, though I wish more people would do their homework and come forward, especially those who have leading roles, not only in the art world, but also in the politics of land use and rural conservation.

When I started writing this short essay, I suspected I would quickly get into the politics behind this poem. Yet I have to say again that they are just that, *behind* the poem – and behind the book which this poem closes. It is a book about loss, and sadness, both in the personal and the wider societal context, a book that opens with a painful, even bitter evocation of my native land, (the first poem in the collection, 'The Fair Chase' was prompted by an invitation from Stuart Kelly to contribute to an anthology he was putting together about Scotland). This poem doesn't unpick or deny the causes of that sense of loss – and of betrayal – but it does move forward into a new terrain where the speaker finds himself 'ready to be persuaded'. That those words are the last in the book is important to me. Given the current climate, I think it is at least part of the work of any artist to analyse and understand what is going wrong and set down responses to that (the articulation of ignored griefs is of huge importance now, and nothing does this better than poetry), but it is also vital that we use that analysis as a starting point for new imaginative ventures, new forays in possibility that – at some magical level, the level of visualisation, if you like – might counter the damage being done by those among us who so lack grace or imagination, (or is it simply the creaturely instinct?) that they are ready to destroy a habitat, or a neighbour's sense of well-being, for something as essentially uninteresting as financial profit. The enormous beauty of the world around us – not just pretty, 'green' 'nature', but the very fact of anything being here at all – is still a cause for celebration, and that is where the poem ends, with the speaker 'dumbstruck', (and so no longer complaining about his aches and pains) and ready to carry on living, in community with his fellow creatures.

From the Chinese

Turn of the year
and a white Christmas turning to slush
on my neighbours' fields,

crows on the high road,
the yard streaked with coal dust
and gritting,

geraniums turning to mush
in the tubs and baskets.

I walk to the end of the road
to ease my sciatica:
ditch water, gorse bones; how did I get so cold

so quickly?

Thaw in the hedge
and the old gods return to the land
as buzzard and pink-footed goose and that

daylong, perpetual scrape
of winter forage;

but this is the time of year
when nothing to see
gives way to the hare in flight, the enormous

beauty of it stark against the mud
and thawglass on the track, before
it darts away, across the open fields

and leaves me dumbstruck, ready to be persuaded.

DUMPERS

John Kinsella

On Long Beach, that ran down one side of the peninsular town, the waves were considered temperamental. Serious surfers rarely bothered, but beginners mingled with body-surfers and boogie-boarders most days whether the surf was 'pumping' or not. It was a wind-driven shore break, without a spot of reef around, so the direction of the wind made all the difference to the shape of the waves. And when it wasn't 'working', Long Beach was a washing machine, a grind of foam and sand and crushing dumpers. It was also notorious for savage rips that would cart swimmers way out into the bay and then on to deep ocean. You would never call it a family beach, but nonetheless, families wandered down over the dunes and spent whole days there on weekends. During the week, other than a few kids wagging school and the odd neophyte surfer willing to take on anything, it was pretty well deserted.

But during the warmest weeks of the school year, the senior sports master, Mr Rush, would walk his upper-school students across the dunes to Long Beach for 'beach activities'. This would include swimming if the water was considered 'safe' enough, as well as beach cricket and volleyball. For two hours on a Thursday afternoon, the Pacific gulls and seagulls would vie with Mr Rush's whistle for attention.

It's difficult to get inside Mr Rush's head. From outside, he seemed a brutal and brutalising man. A Korean War veteran who, though nearing retirement, was in perfect shape, with the body of a man twenty years younger, he unsurprisingly encouraged and protected his sports stars, and was harsh with the failures. He would turn a blind eye to hazing, and would laugh with his stars about the pathetic flailing of the 'weaklings'. Yet there was more to him than this, and even the weaklings who suffered under his reign knew it, and feared him all the more for it.

Some of them suspected he despised the stars even more than he despised them. They couldn't say how or why. It was something to do with the way he stared at them, looked at them when the stars weren't around; the occasional impatient gesture of hand lifting from hip to indicate something was *almost* right.

Andy Bright was one of the 'weaklings'. Because he was mediocre at his studies, but capable of being top of the class if motivated enough, he was nicknamed 'Brighty'. Maybe they would have called him Brighty anyway. It seems the default setting. Though not a total failure at sports, he wasn't well built, and was a late developer, that greatest sin among boys. But if he liked a sport he could do well enough to avoid a pummelling from the 'stars', who might still grab his balls in the changing rooms where he tried to change under a towel close to the door (escape hatch) as quickly as possible.

On one occasion Dag and Mutt, the two star full-forwards of the school, had dragged him out of the change-rooms semi-naked and dumped him in front of the girls' change-rooms, watching as he writhed in humiliation. The girls didn't actually laugh much, though Mr Rush grabbed him by the ear and dragged him back. That was justice Mr Rush style.

However, Brighty didn't mind sports on beach days, finding he could run around a bit, splash a bit, and generally muck around under the radar with the other weaklings. Mr Rush wasn't such a hard nut on beach days, though you wouldn't think this if you walked past. He still blew his whistle insanely and yelled abuse

JOHN KINSELLA
© Tracy Ryan

at boys who were faltering. You'd also notice his crew cut, the zinc cream on his face like war paint, the shorts so tight it was clear he'd carefully arranged his prominent 'bits'. On the beach he took his shirt off like all the boys, and across his back was a tattoo that said *Mum*. Years earlier, when one of the sporty boys had joked with Mr Rush about this, the consequences had been so extreme that the legend kept in check whatever people even half-thought about it. It was never mentioned.

Hey, Brighty, catch this!

Brighty turned round and caught a sand-ball right in the face. Mutt laughed, calling to Dag to come and look at Brighty trying to get the sand out of his eyes.

Some of the other boys laughed. Brighty laughed as well – best method of defence – and plunged into the surf to get the sand out of his hair. Since it was grinding hard that day, he got more sand in than out. Because it was rough, the boys had been told to stay within five metres of the shore. On a perfect day, the waves would break right and occasionally form crystalline green tubes, but today they were tumbling head over heels and breaking at irregular points along their crests. It was a mess. The wind was switching directions and the sand on the beach occasionally flew into hair and eyes anyway. Brighty wasn't worried.

He heard Dag calling to Mutt, Go out and give the scrawny little bastard a dunking.

Even that didn't worry Brighty. Though he was small, he was a good swimmer. Not a certificate-good swimmer, but an untrained sort of swimmer, very familiar with the ocean and with Long Beach in particular. He knew its moods. His older brother Ben was a shit-hot surfer. A school drop-out, jobless and into pot, he was another reason Brighty copped it from the sports stars. His brother was a well-known 'lost-cause'. But he could surf, really surf. Sometimes he took Brighty out with him when Long Beach was working. Brighty had a long plank of a board, and could only just stand up, but he always enjoyed himself.

Go on Mutt, get out after him! Dag was getting frantic.

Brighty moved a little further out, just in case. He kept one eye on Mr Rush who would eat him alive for going out that far, but Mr Rush had combined whistling and playing and joined in the volleyball. Brighty thought Mr Rush looked like he was having heaps of fun.

Then Mutt was running into the surf and lurching straight for him.

Brighty watched him approach. He could study Mutt closely because time had slowed down. Mutt was a handsome beast. A good six-four, sculpted muscles, already a few curls of black hair on his broad chest. And Mutt wasn't stupid, though he pretended to be so. He was a top maths student, even if a bottom English student. Mutt wore pink board-shorts because he could get away with wearing pink board-shorts. No one was going to call *him* a poof.

The afternoon sun cast a halo in the spray around his hair as he splashed and furrowed his way through the surf to where Brighty was treading water, bobbing among the dumpers. Brighty was ducking down as each dumper closed over, and managing to stay out of the washing machine. That was years of practice.

Mutt was close to Brighty now, but a dumper closed over and sent arms and limbs flailing. Mutt emerged coughing and spluttering and angry. He staggered back to shore to find Dag laughing at him.

Get the little bastard, Mutt, get out there! And Mutt went back for more and got dumped again.

Brighty hung out just beyond the break. He kept an eye on Mr Rush, who was still too absorbed in spiking the volleyball into one of the student's legs to notice anything. Mr Rush was in a state of bliss.

Then suddenly Mutt was out near Brighty again. He'd snagged a break in the dumpers and got through, and was flailing at Brighty, who swam deftly out a few more strokes. Brighty felt the cold, then the pull of the rip, instantly. He was just on the edge of it and drew away just in time. But Mutt went straight into its throat. Within seconds he was being dragged out to deep water. He was tired through struggling with the dumpers, and Brighty could see that Mutt wasn't a strong swimmer. Muscle, but no savvy. Mutt was drowning.

Brighty didn't hesitate: he swam into the mouth of the rip. I am Jonah, he told himself. He was afraid but hyped, and swam with the rip until he reached Mutt. Next to Mutt he felt tiny. He felt his cock and balls shrivel even smaller as he collided with the school giant.

Grab my arm, Mutt. Brighty was going to sidestroke his way across the rip. Mutt was gurgling and flailing, and his wheeling arms struck Brighty so hard that they momentarily stunned him. They went out further with the rip, and Brighty himself started to swallow water and choke. Mutt was big and heavy and dragging him down. He was trying to climb on Brighty and use him as a life-raft. Brighty pushed him off and ducked under to grab Mutt around the neck and shoulders. Just lie on your back and kick your feet, Mutt!

Then Mutt gave way and his body relaxed, and he went with Brighty.

Exhausted, Brighty lifted his head out of the water as they broke the edge of the rip and saw all the kids standing at the edge of the surf. Mr Rush was there, blowing his whistle and pointing out to sea. By the time Brighty had dragged Mutt to the dumpers, Mr Rush was in there too. The dumpers broke around Mr Rush as if he were ancient granite that had been bashed and battered by waves for thousands of years. He wrested Mutt from Brighty and said, You'll make it back in from here, son. With that, he took Mutt the rest of the way to shore, where he gave him mouth-to-mouth.

Mutt was okay. Just sheepish. Not even Dag risked a joke. The class trudged back over the dunes to the school with Brighty dragging behind. No one had said a word to him. They steered clear. He repelled them.

Back at school, Brighty walked carefully into the change-room. He passed Dag, who had flung Brighty's bag across the floor.

Don't say anything about Mutt to anyone, you little bitch!

Brighty grabbed his bag and went to his place near the door, where he changed under his towel. He flinched, waiting for one of the stars to rip it away. Mr Rush had taken Mutt to the nurse's room, but everyone knew Mutt was fine. That was just the rules.

And then, when Brighty was walking away from the change-room and from the day, he heard Mr Rush's whistle.

Hey Bright, I want a word with you.

He stood and waited because Mr Rush was coming to him. Mr Rush said, You learn in your life that some things never happen, son. No one will thank you. No one will say jack-shit if you keep your mouth shut. And that's the best way, son. The best way. That's the pain – the pain of bottling it up – that'll keep you going. Get you up day after day ready to start again. You'll never shine on the field – never. Mutt will, because he's a star.

Brighty watched Mr Rush walk crisply back towards his fiefdom. There was a heap of homework due in the next day, and he thought about heading over to the library. But then he kicked at the ground and thought, Nah… think I'll go hang out with my brother. He's always good for a laugh when he's stoned. And he won't be doing much else today – the surf's shit.

DAVID
CONSTANTINE

24

DAVID CONSTANTINE

A Faiyum death mask

We in our own and local fashion having had
A Cydnus, an arrival, refuse to be shipped off
Faceless under the wraps of death. Love said to me
Slot under the lattice of the bandages a mask
Of her, as true as the arts can make it to the look
She wore when by the river's flood tide she was landed
Here on the shores of the life that you had lived till then
Without her. Show her still and for ever looking up
Alert and curious, taking in your welcome
So that when she berths alone in the unsmiling place
And cannot breathe a word the receivers there will pause
And read her face and marvel at you both precisely.

Faiyum is a district of Middle Egypt where many Romano-Egyptian
mummy portraits have been found.

Enotria
Tomba 736, una donna, VI secolo a. C.

Lady, in the rubble of you, in among
The unstrung vertebrae and bits of rib
And in the vacancy of sex and womb
And either side your skull which looks as frail
As a sea urchin denuded by the sun
Ivory, gold and amber are lasting well
And even iron that rusts, an iron key
Still lies intact where your absent right hand
Had grasped it, woman, female of the human
Species, shape in the dirt, much like a form
Of life that sank into extinction down
To a bed of mud and under centuries
Of drifting silt and under millions
Of pressing rock, so many millions
Of years and more, upheaving and eroding
Till your poor slice of time comes back to light
And a fellow human stares (as though this were
The worst of it) at your missing hand and feels
You left a grief behind that could not bear
To think you'd go where you would not be loved
And dressed you again for sovereignty
In the gifts he had given you, in amber
Ivory, filigree gold, the earrings,
Loops of necklace, low slung belt, and closed your hand
On the key to some fit lodging, lady.

Enotria = Œnotria [wine-land], a district of Southern Italy [roughly
modern Basilicata] much settled by the Ancient Greeks.

Red on black

I am told this flat land is a vast necropolis
And knowing that, I find it hard to sleep.
The idea works in the earth of me. Like most
Who lie awake I want continuation.

Often at night I think of the Bologna stone.
Lay it for a while in a good strong sun
Shut in the dark then it will shine for hours.
That is its way of breathing in the world:

Give me a deal of sun I will intake it
Husband it in me and give it out again with increase
In places where the very idea of light has gone from mind.
Even more like that are the red-figure vases

Laid up in the tombs for the lucky in life
In the hope their spent warmth would continue
Red on black, their walking together and conversing
Eros and music, episodes from the stories

Shining and tuneful as the constellations.
Often at night my thoughts turn to the looters:
Out of the silent tumuli hereabouts
As from a long-lost kiln they lifted vases

Cold to the touch, the fired beauties,
Delivered them into the continuing sun
The lovers, the singers, the flute players, the dancers
Red on black, cold, cold, outlived by fired clay.

Bologna stone is a phosphorescent form of barite [barium sulphate]
first found near Bologna in the seventeenth century.

Salerno Cathedral
Roman sarcophagus of a man and wife

Dressed marble slabs, four walls, a floor, a lid
Fitted together tight, harder than bone
Hard and implacable as the summons that
The messenger, light as a swallow, swooped

Under their lintel with. Brute marble fact
How they have softened it! How languidly
He poses leaning on his dipped-out torch
Two of him (there are two of them) and how

Within that frame, between those minders, stone,
A frieze, is moved to impersonate the sea
All running, curling, not one level line,
The dance and effervescence of the sea

Lifting for a festival: women astride
Horn-blowing tritons, naked, tugging the drenched
Beard round to have the mouth or sliding down
The chute of fish-coils, sea facilitating

The squirms of scale and skin, and flighted cupids
Showing them in mirrors. The buried pair
Unlidded long ago, blown down the winds,
Thanks be to them now for their furious horns

The squeals of Eros undulant through warm blood
The roar and bubbling of the sea. Observing
Love's fluid mutiny against the fact
Nonchalant Hermes surely envies them.

Manchester Museum
Cast of a woman of Pompeii

The woman of Pompeii again, another cast of her
Cast of the mould that was all that remained of her
After the fire and centuries in a stratum where
She dematerialised, exactly vacating her shape
That could be cast. Her only visitor, coming upon her

Here in a hush, it troubled me: she is reproducible
Like any statue, the woman prone, pillowing her head
Coiffured, on her right arm; the sleeve, left elbow, torn;
Tatters of the dress between her shoulder blades; below
All stripped; the woman whose form, the living lines

Of her, from heel to head the soft ash copied close
And shrouded hard. In the present tense of memory
She troubles me. Turn over now, I said, just so, curving
A little left, legs parted a little, and pulled a pillow
Under your belly, cool, just so, the slopes, the dip

And rise, parting your legs, I knelt a moment there
Viewing the line of you, so beautiful, your face
Hiding on your right arm. In a moment
You'll hear my heart on you and feel against the beat
Of your blood at the temple mine through your ruffled hair.

A love of churches

At sixteen I switched to Early Communion
Because it was shorter, but soon quitted for good
Because, like Saint Anthony
I could not keep my mind off the doings of the night before
But I never did lose my love of churches

Large and small but especially the small
Crouched low among their graves and however ancient
Predated by their yews, the font
Tapping deep into Terra, the nested corbels
Still exhibiting every degree of scurrility

And capitals, pews and choir stalls affirming the faith
In mermaids, centaurs, undines, green men
Whose eloquent gobs run over
Into boundless foliage. And now
Here's another house I could worship in Sunday mornings

And not renounce Saturday nights: that column
Garlanded in a rising or descending spiral
Pushing up through a helix of scallops
Is cold stone, but give me your hand
Let me fit the sunrise, the comb, the mound to your palm

Slope your long fingers down over the promontory
Feel the stone warm, my palmer
Many ancient ways are still new to us
There is much still to learn setting out from a place like this
Where the sea licks the windows.

INTERVIEW

THOUGHTS FROM A STORY HOUSE

David Fickling talks to Angela Macmillan

David Fickling is a children's book editor and publisher. In 1999 he set up David Fickling Books, a small story house in Oxford which is now an imprint of Random House. DFB authors include Philip Pullman, Mark Haddon, John Boyne and Siobhan Dowd.

David Fickling Comics publishes **The Phoenix**, *a weekly story comic.*

http://www.davidficklingbooks.com
http://www.thephoenixcomic.co.uk

Were you read to as a child? Were there books in your house?

No, not really. There were books. My mother read a lot of popular novels – she was a reader in that lovely sense that she read what she liked. She would have read all the *Poldark* books. I was one of five brothers so we had books such as Hammond Innes. My father died when I was twelve but I found some books of his, Dylan Thomas and John Cowper Powys, but books weren't a big deal. I was lucky that it wasn't a *no*-books house and I was a member of the library. I remember loving the library and the way of choosing books, the mooching, those hops you make as a young reader – the fantastic opportunity to borrow and try. I really liked that great freedom – not you have got to read *this*, but rather 'I'll try this because that other one really worked'. The library encouraged me to branch out because things were cheek-by-jowl, and I discovered science fiction. [Cackles]

DAVID
FICKLING

So you were mooching alone, no one helped you…

I would never have asked. I was deaf to people even if they gave me good advice, though I probably *was* helped by people when I did not know they were helping. Things were put in my way without my realising it. But I would have been off-put by too-obvious advice. The library was 'it' as far as I was concerned and that flowed from the miracle of *finding* what I was reading.

People are often very nostalgic about their childhood reading. I thought I would get criticism in A Little, Aloud *for leaving out someone's essential children's book. I wondered what books were most important for you?*

I was given no sense of what I should (or should not) read and that was the most enormous blessing. Because I had no prior sense of what was good or bad, I had to make up my own mind. There were some very special books, which the world might not think were special at all. I remember my first Enid Blyton, a book called *The Boy Next Door*, probably the first book I ever read apart from learning to read. I was bored stiff of learning to read. *Janet and John* (the reading scheme I learnt on) was in my head a strange geometry of which I did not know the code or cypher. I remember the sense of weirdness – that reading was separate from books. And I remember clearly the competition in the classroom for who was on *Red Book* 2, or whatever, that sense that other people were on different books and that was called 'reading'. Weird. So finding *The Boy Next Door* was a kind of miracle, a bomb going off in my head. I never had any taste, I just read what my brain responded to and that was lucky.

Did you try and replicate this approach with your own children?

The best way is for the reader to want to find it for themselves. I wanted my children to be readers; it was the most important thing as a parent I should be doing for them, but I really struggled with *how* to do it. I also thought it was a bit of a curse that I was working in books and loved them so much because the biggest problem is the misunderstanding of where anyone is in their reading development at any one time. It is possible to give someone things that are incredibly good but that they can't see at that time, and that is so off-putting. That is the one major mistake made in teaching reading – the desire on the teacher's part to 'bring the person on'. It is important to put books in the child's path but how it is put in the path is also vital. I made the mistake early on of trying to get my children to read things and then realised that that was too pressurised and they didn't trust me. There is a lack of trust involved in a situation where you know the person means you well; you do not trust it's the truth. It is like your Mum saying 'You look lovely'. Not believable!

Has your career always been in books for children?

Yes, but I did not have a plan. I instinctively loved story, narrative. But it is absolutely clear to me that the book stays the same but the reader changes. As Heraclitus says, you can't step in the same river twice. I re-read *Madame Bovary* recently, having first read it when I was about twenty-one. I remembered it as being slightly romantic. I had thought: *she'd* be someone I'd like to know; silly boring doctor husband – his fault. I read it again aged 55 and it nearly blew my head off; I was utterly shocked and all but had a nervous breakdown because it is about the dangers of romancing. I imagine there are people who could read it at twenty-one and totally get it. This is a tale about my slowness, not about the novel. I loved reading *Madame Bovary* again and realising that I was reading a different book. You asked me if I have always been in children's books and I would say I have always been in *story*. I am a bit bemused by the children's library ticket and the adult library ticket because as a child I did not find a problem about wandering into the adult section. What led me there were authors who were in both places. I needed bridges. Arthur C. Clarke was one of my bridges. The publishing company has the same lack of understanding of the difference between an adult book and a children's book.

Was there a sense of mission in the desire for your own publishing house?

Mission is probably the wrong word, too purposeful. I think there is a kind of simplicity, if not a simpleton, at the heart of recognition. That has to be *you* recognising – you can't recognise on behalf of other people. If I try to give an explanation for publishing, it is that if I saw something that made my heart beat faster then why wouldn't that work for anybody else? But these are conscious thoughts I am having now; I don't think I had a sense of mission at all. I wanted to be associated with stories, I wanted to be working with them, to be close to the makers, just like any reader. There is something mesmerising about brilliant storytelling and it is natural to how we convey everything that matters. I think stories are central to our existence. I would characterise David Fickling Books as a storyhouse.

*I have had an extraordinary year of reading for the anthology (**A Little, Aloud for Children**). My youngest is nearly 30 so I have been away from children's books for a long time. But coming afresh to the new stories, I have been impressed by the depth and the seriousness of content as well as the fun and joy. I think all adults could do with a year of such reading.*

I couldn't agree more and I would absolutely say that children's literature is not a matter of shallow entertainment; it is a matter of resonant depth and a beckoning on by the bird on the branch in the dark forest going deeper and deeper. The very finest children's books are massively resonant for readers of all ages. It doesn't surprise me that a brilliant book for an eight-year-old should also continue to resonate and reverberate for a fifty-year-old. They are the finest books. The simplicity, warmth, elegance, and the humour are some of the very finest things in world literature.

*In a century where most comics have disappeared could you explain your decision to publish **The Phoenix**? I can remember as a child sitting by the gate impatiently waiting for my weekly comic to arrive. It was a hugely important part of my childhood. There were no other girls my age in my road but I swapped **Eagle** or **Beano**, **Dandy**, **Topper** with the boys and my **Girl** was secretly rather popular.*

As a boy I was in a state of excitement about comics. My brother had *The Swift* and mine was *Harold Hare*. I can barely remember the comic in detail. It seemed very big to me and it was Mine. The important thing, having four brothers, is that it was something that was not held in common. I only remember reading delight in comics, and I swear that if I know anything at all about the editing of story, at least half of it came from comics, the sheer excitement and the variety and imagination. I want to stress that publishing *The Phoenix* is not a nostalgic, sentimental impulse. It is wanting to recreate the excitement and to have that available. At one time, there were 40 or 50 comics, and it was a time when boys' interests and girls' interests were heavily marked – and your peers were the strongest demarcators. These demarcations are now being lost, I think, but back then I know I was just as interested in the story values of 'The Four Marys' as I was in 'Dan Dare'. Comics introduced me to *every* variety of story. This way of reading by strip I learnt naturally at the age of five in *Harold Hare*. It was unpressured reading – there was no one saying 'You have got to learn to read' but I wanted to do it because there the comic was, it was for me, and I knew that I owned it.

So as a publisher interested in storytelling, the comic is just another form. I believe, though I haven't done any research, that the fall-off in reading is largely a consequence of the absent-minded loss of our comics industry. I want to re-create that universe of relaxed reading for fun. Really it is the comic illustrators and storytellers who are *doing* it, but I want to help. The whole idea of *The Phoenix* is a seed for comics to come flooding back so that children can have them in childhood as a right.

Comics were about nothing but reading for pleasure. I'll give you an example, there used to be a comic called *Look and Learn*. In the back of it was a strip called 'The Trigan Empire'. Now I was as curious as any little boy, but I never used to read the *Look and Learn* bit, only 'The Trigan Empire'. It was by a guy called Don Lawrence (as I found out later). It was brilliant telling and it was epic, and mythic about Romans in spaceships; it led me to the sense of wide, grand horizons. Nowadays I like to think of things I would like to have met in my childhood and didn't, such as The Moomins, I'd love to have met The Moomins.

On your website you say that your books 'work'.

the PHOENIX

THE WEEKLY STORY COMIC

ISSUE NO. 28
4 July 2012

£2.99

9 772048 827000

Return of THE Star Cat!

TROY ON THE TRAIL!

OPENING AUSTEN'S COFFIN!

© James Turner

That is a big claim; a really big boast.

When I talk to our project workers whose job it is to read with children, they tell me that one of your most reliable books – and what I mean by that is one that can be relied upon to 'work' – is **The London Eye Mystery** *by Siobhan Dowd. What did you first spot in this book?*

Siobhan Dowd was the most miraculous author I ever met. Maybe it is all sharpened in my memory by the fact that she tragically died about four years after I met her. She was the most naturally gifted person; a publisher's dream. Not in a sentimental way for she was a very intelligent truth-telling, funny-spirited person and I know she had come to writing late after being a huge figure in PEN, that she supported Roma writing, and then suddenly she started writing. I asked her if this was to do with getting cancer and she said absolutely not. She delivered four novels, which I think are peerless. After I had read her first, *A Swift Pure Cry*, she said 'Surely you can think of something to say editorially about it', but I couldn't think of a thing. You feel really stupid when you can't think of anything that would improve a book but Siobhan was a writer above my pay grade. Luckily I met a friend of hers, Helen Graves, who has a bat-squeak editorial ability and she did help Siobhan. I am not being self-deprecating. I could literally just recognise it and enjoy it.

You asked me about Siobhan's *The London Eye Mystery.* It's not very difficult for me to read a book and recognise it. That is what I mean by working. It is not just a gut thing, reading is both gut and brain. That's what reading makes you do – really *think* – so I am thinking all the way through and finding that at the heart of it there is what they used to call a 'locked room mystery' and she is able to do this, as well as width and humour and enjoyment, and it works for me. It's not hard to recognise these stories. The difficulty starts when you start to second guess yourself: Would teachers like that? Would adults like that? But here I had a natural advantage because I had never had the critical thing laid over me. I just ask 'Does it work?' And then there's the sense that you know that when you read it again it will *still* work and will give off more each time. Where does that come from? I think you can sense that storehouse quality when you are reading something really good for the first time. It is a hugely privileged position to be an editor – it's like being at the library and discovering something brilliant behind a nondescript red cover. I remember feeling excited by the book but you have to remember I had published two novels by her already.

The most original things to me are not marginal things, they are not on the edge; they are right in the middle of the eye, and at the centre of things, and they look as if they have always been, so they have a kind of eternity about them. I had the same feeling reading Philip Pullman's *Northern Lights*, as if it had always been. The most original things remake the world. I can't *imagine* the world without Sherlock Holmes yet he was invented by Conan Doyle, I know he is part of a tradition but Sherlock Holmes is a making and that's how I feel about *The London Eye Mystery*.

What I am trying to recognise as an editor are those things that will work for any reader, particularly for children where if they have something put in front of them that doesn't work it is massively off-putting for the whole process. There is a huge responsibility to publish books but not to force things into the hands of readers, things that are going to turn them off for ever.

A lot of books for young readers these days are 'issue' led, even picture books for the very young. What do you say to parents who say why introduce children so early to all that is ugly and unhappy and even evil in an adult world when time as a child is so comparatively short.

It's hard to answer. The thing I learnt in the library was Don't judge a book by its cover, Don't judge a book by its subject and I would apply that to issue books as well. There are various different views of childhood that are prevalent in the culture. I have a sense that before the Victorians there wasn't really a sense of childhood at all. Then with the Victorians, in came books and chap books and the sense of a paradise-like childhood for certain rich kids where childhood has to be protected, and in this protected childhood you can only read certain things and they have to be wholesome, not bad for you; but then that perspective is turned round by an argument that says we must equip children for life because life is harsh. But it is completely against how I learnt to read and how I think most people learn the joy of reading. There is no joy in reading about dreadful or over-programmatic issues. One of the things about stories is that they should not carry a *definite meaning*, so an issue book is, by its very nature, anti-story. Even though I love things such as *Pilgrim's Progress*, I like them when I am *not thinking* about their programmatic nature. As a child, I really enjoyed the *Narnia* books. When I later discovered they were about Christianity, it stalled me. If I had known they were telling me about Christianity while I was reading them, that would have put me off because I was being instructed. Actually I think C. S. Lewis is a very good storyteller.

The great storytellers – the great writers – understand the pressing nature of the truth; they place you in positions where your mind is reaching forward.

What you called earlier 'the beckoning on'.

Yes, a beckoning on because you yourself are being led by the story: 'What does this mean?', 'What would I do?', these are all thoughts where you are *there*. And you know how loyal those thoughts are. Reading is an invitation to think and if you reach for the issue you close down the thinking and the creativity in your own head, and the dialogue between the author and you. The best stories are not ones where the writer excludes the reader from the book but the ones that include you, where the story is completed by the reader reading it. Many writers have different ways of talking about this and sometimes they want it to be a mystery to them as well, they will say things like 'my characters took control'.

Like Dickens…

Yes, the very best writers, and so that story is a shared thing – not the writer saying 'I am Lord and Master', and not the reader saying 'I am the student'. I think it is lazy to reach for instruction. You are not drawn in, you are taking down notes and while there is a place for taking down notes, story is not the place.

MATTHEW HOWARD

Reed Bunting
25th February, Sutton Fen

The earliest singers are best, the first
with the keenest eye. Of all these hectares
of reed, this singer points the truest
territory relative to his range;

knows this is everything they will need
for the season. Sure, he has no call to riff,
just persists in the brief form of his song.
Perched on a gnarled dead alder,

here is his pitch. *Go with him*. He will raise
a cup nestled with a tangle of bog myrtle –
it will fill through hurtling draughts of sun and rain
yet hold here, then brim with keener eyes.

Ascension Day 2008
For Joseph

The hedgerow bursts in commotion
as we pass; a magpie, beak-yolked,
needle in the female blackbird's agitation,
skulks off to the back field. I lose her.
But you have seen the toppled nest,
the yolk-spatter in the grassy ditch below.
Your face cracks before I can catch it.
I try telling you that this is spring
and we will still hear blackbirds singing
tomorrow. But you, not yet four,
you can only see today and these eggs.
So I say how the magpie is much-maligned,
much more than black and white, how he's princely
in his gleaming blue and coppery green
and how he loves his lady for life;
how it has to be, not all eggs laid can sing.
'There! Magpie!' you say, your eyes drying,
pointing me to the hawthorn's crown-top
all leafed and near full-flowering:
a flick of his tail and he's off. You're smiling
and I catch the bounce-back of that supple branch,
from the weight of what was and what is.
You take my hand and we walk on.

THE RISE EXPERIENCE

JACKIE KAY'S VISIT TO HMP STYAL

Charlie Darby-Villis meets Jackie Kay

I n October, during Manchester Literature Festival, Jackie Kay read to an audience of women prisoners at HMP Styal as part of the RISE project (Reading in Secure Environments). This Arts Council-funded project is a collaboration between The Reader Organisation and six literature festivals across the country. We invite poets and authors to participate in the public festival and also to put on an event in a secure setting in the festival area. As part of Durham Book Festival, Jean Sprackland and Michael Stewart visited HMP Low Newton; American poet Philip Schultz read at HMP Kennet as part of Sefton Celebrates Writing; during the Manchester Literature Festival, Jackie Kay went to Styal, Joe Dunthorne visited a Manchester Probation Trust-approved premises, while Inua Ellams read with young men at the Gardiner Unit at Prestwich Hospital.

Each of the secure settings holds at least one reading group every week, and readers from these groups made up the core of the audience for the readings. The project aims to encourage those already in the group as well as to promote the group to the rest of the closed community. But it is much more than that. It acts as a bridge between the *closed* community of the prison or secure ward and the community *outside*. In the reading groups I hold in prison I am constantly reminded of the power of literature to connect people to each other. It is important that RISE is part of mainstream literature festivals. The events in the secure settings are conceived and presented as normal festival events, albeit in an unusual location, and as an integral part of the festival, not an 'outreach' or 'education' project. The secure audience is aware that they are part of something going on in the outside world, that connections exist between them and the wider community. In the words of one woman prisoner, 'It makes me feel part of society again'. This link is also made clear to public audiences in festival brochures and often highlighted by the writer too, keen to share the experience of their secure visit.

THE INTERVIEW

HMP Styal is a women's prison on the outskirts of Manchester, holding women of all ages and backgrounds. Fifty of these women gathered in the chapel to hear Jackie Kay read. It was a lively and warm occasion, 'beautifully inspiring', as one woman said. Jackie read from her poetry and her memoir *Red Dust Road*, and the women greeted the reading by turn with raucous belly laughs and with absolute rapt silence, at times holding each other's hands while listening with an intensity you could almost see. Afterwards the buzz in the room was palpable, the excited, purposeful chatter of people talking to each other about what they've just been part of, fifty people talking about great writing. I was able to ask Jackie a few questions about her visit.

Have you read in a criminal justice or a secure mental health setting before?

I have read at Cookham Woods, done workshops for a month with lifers in Wormwood Scrubs and also been in Holloway Prison twice, once with a play of mine, and once to read from *Red Dust Road*.

RISE did feel very different. The whole environment felt more easy – and people in there seemed more attentive and less pressured than people I've seen in other prisons. It was as if the prison itself had a different ethos.

I accepted the invitation because I always find working in prisons thought-provoking and rewarding in some way. People inside think often very philosophically, and that way of thinking is invaluable for a writer. I always go in with an open mind. My first job is to get people's attention, usually. But in Styal, that was easy and everybody was already prepared to listen and be interested. I felt uplifted by the response of the women.

How did you choose what to read?

I wanted work that might resonate. I chose *Red Dust Road,* my memoir, because it is my own story, and I imagined the women would find that more interesting. I also wanted to give them a preview of something nobody had yet seen so I read my new anti-racist football poem 'Here's my Pitch' in Styal before I read it to the Sheffield United Stadium on the Monday. I also read my poem 'Darling' about the loss of a friend, because most people have lost somebody and identify with that. I think if my work can hold up a mirror to somebody's life even if it is just to think 'I've felt like that before. I know what that feels like' then I feel it's been worth something.

I always think about where I am and what to read in relation to where I am and I always try and tailor my selection to the people I'm reading to. So if I'm reading to people on the isle of Shetland or Arran, I might read a knitting poem! All of the work I read at Styal I would choose to read at any public event.

Did you find any differences or similarities in the response of the secure and public audiences?

I found the questions different in some ways. People give more of themselves inside. They tell you something of themselves first. Somebody said at Styal that she had never found her father or been told who he was. People when they ask questions in public don't necessarily feel they have to give something (although sometimes some of them do). Often people will ask more naked questions in secure environments. Once a woman asked me why I was defending my birth father when he'd been so horrible to me. She asked me if it was my pride that was making me do that.

Nobody had ever asked before and it made me think for weeks! Another time a woman asked if I could finish the chapter I was reading from because 'I'm getting out tomorrow', which was sad and funny at the same time. It made me think perhaps she'd be more likely to read inside a secure environment than she would out. And once a woman wanted me to write an identical message for her son as I wrote for her so that they could have the same thing on their walls. That really moved me. It also made me think that people in secure environments have to have a kind of parallel life where the people outside live alongside them in some sort of way, and where they are often having to *imagine* what that life is like. In that way, there are connections and similarities with the life of a writer who also is always interested in parallel lives in the roads not taken, in the shadow life, if you like.

Many of the women who attended your event at Styal said that they identified with you, had a feeling that you've been 'through it'. What difference, if any, do you think this makes?

It makes a big difference if people feel you are no stranger to hurt and rejection, and if you can find a way to be honest about that without being self-pitying. All of us have had difficult times. Some people deal with that by building a reserve around them, a protective wall. I find my strength in being open about difficult things and I find it reassuring and uplifting when people respond in kind.

Did you have a creative response to the reading?

Yes, it made me think a lot, particularly about the thought people in secure environments give to the people outside of them. The impact from such a visit can go on inside me for months and the creative response might take a while to come out, but is bubbling merrily away. I'd like to thank the women for being so responsive and kind to me and giving me their whole attention. I won't forget it. Nor their encouragement about reading the football poem and their reflective 'It will go OK and if it doesn't you'll know about it!' I'd be happy to come again!

JACKIE KAY

© Denise Else

47

THE EXTRACT

When Jackie read the opening of her memoir *Red Dust Road* (published by Picador) to the women at Styal, there was laughter when her beautiful Glasgow accent shifted easily into that of Nigerian man as she recounted her first meeting with her birth father. She lulled the audience with the security of humour until the sucker-punch: she was his shame made flesh; he was saved but she was his sin. Now there was total silence in the room, the silence of absolute concentration. This is where some of the women held hands. There are nods and shared smiles as Jackie continues to describe telling her father she's a lesbian, which change to shrieks of laughter as she reveals his salacious response.

I'm about to have a conversation with my birth father for the first time.

Jonathan is moving about from foot to foot, shifting his weight from side to side, like a man who is about to say something life-changing. He begins: 'Before we can proceed with this meeting, I would like to pray for you and to welcome you to Nigeria.' I feel alarmed. Extreme religion scares the hell out of me. It seems to me like a kind of madness. But it is obvious to me that Jonathan won't be able to talk at all if I try and skip the sermon. So I say, 'OK, then,' and he says, 'Sit, please.' And I sit.

He plucks the Bible from the plastic bag. Then he immediately starts whirling and twirling around the blue hotel room, dancing and clapping his hands above his head, then below his waist, pointing his face up at the ceiling and then down to the floor, singing, 'O God Almighty, O God Almighty, O God Almighty, we welcome Jackie Kay to Nigeria. Thank you, God Almighty, for bringing her here safely. She has crossed the waters. She has landed on African soil for the very first time. O God Almighty!' He does some fancy footwork. He is incredibly speedy for a man of seventy-three. He's whirling like a dervish. Suddenly, he takes off his shoes and puts them on my bed and kneels on the floor and reads the first of many extracts from the Bible. He seems to half read and half recite them; he appears to know the Bible by heart. As he recites he looks at me directly, quite a charming look, slightly actorish. The sermon for him is a kind of performance; his whole body gets thrown into it.

'God has given you this talent. You are a writer. You have written books. You have been blessed. God already knows about you. Don't think for a second that God hasn't been waiting for you. Now all you must do is receive Christ and your talent will become even bigger and you will become more focused. Amen. From this moment on you are protected. God protects the talented. Amen. You can walk through fire, you won't get burnt. You can swim in dangerous waters, you won't drown. Don't even bother with your hotel safe. God is looking out for you.'

I shift uneasily in my seat. Christ Almighty, my father is barking mad. He spins and dances and sings some more, singing in the most God-awful flat voice, really off-key. The singing sounds like a mixture of African chanting and hymns. It's a shock. Despite the fact that he can't sing, his performance is captivating. I watch his bare feet dance round the room and recognize my own toes. He looks over directly into my eyes again to see if I'm persuaded. 'I see in your eyes that you are not yet able to put your full trust in God. And yet you know that that would make me happy. At every reading you do, you could take the message of our Lord. Think of the people you could convert.' (I think of the twelve people at a reading in Milton Keynes Central Library on a rainy Thursday night.)

'Think of all the people you could bring to the Lord if you get ready to receive Christ.' I look as noncommittal as possible. I start to think that I should try and get this to stop. It feels like a kind of assault. He senses me thinking this and says, 'Just one more extract from the Bible. I prayed to God you would be attentive and you are being attentive. I prayed to God you would be patient and you are being patient.'

He wants me to be cleansed, cleansed of his past sin. 'If animal blood can cleanse sins under the Old Law, how much more can the blood of Jesus Christ cleanse us and prepare us for glory?' As Jonathan says this, his eyes seem to light up from behind like a scary Halloween mask. 'For if the blood of bulls and of goats, and the ashes of a heifer sprinkling the unclean, sanctify the purifying of the flesh, how much more shall the blood of Christ, who through the eternal Spirit offered himself without spot to God, purge your conscience from dead works to serve the living God?'

I realize with a fresh horror that Jonathan is seeing me as the sin, me as impure, me the bastard, illegitimate. I am sitting here, evidence of his sinful past, but I am the sinner, the live embodiment of his sin. He's moved on now, he's a clean man, a man of glory and of God, but I'm sitting on the hotel room chair little better than a whore in his eyes, dirty and unsaved, the living proof of sin.

[…]

'You can tell me. I am your father,' he urges, winningly. It is the first time he has said this simple sentence. He sees it working and repeats it with extra condiments. 'I am your father; you can tell me anything. I love you and I accept you because I am your father. There can be nothing that would shock me.'

It is the first time too that he has appeared really interested in anything about me. Just my luck. Not in my son, not in my childhood, not in my university days, not in my books, not in my parents, but in my *sex drive*! Fucking brilliant. 'Well, you know the woman you spoke to on the telephone?'

'Yes, yes, yes.'

'Well… she's my partner.'

'What do you mean?'

'She's my partner.'

'How so?'

'She's my lover. We've been together for fifteen years.' (I don't bother telling him that just before I flew to Nigeria, Carol Ann told me she didn't love me any more and wanted our relationship to end. Too complicated.)

'Oh-oh, oh-oh, oh-oh, oh-oh you mean you are lesbian?' He credits the word lesbian with three syllables with the emphasis on the last. *Les be an.* You mean you are *les be AN?*'

'Yes, that's right, I'm a lesbian.' Despite myself, I'm agog to see how he will take this news.

'OK-OK-OK-OK, OK-OK-OK-OK,' he says a string of OKs like

prayer beads. Then very quickly he says, 'OK, OK. Which one of you is the man?'

'Sorry?' I say.

'I've often wondered about this,' he says. 'And I have never understood. How does it work? Which one of you is the man?' His eyes have acquired a sleazy shimmer. He is clearly having more fun than he's had all day. 'How is it possible for two women to have sex?' he asks me, asking me perhaps the most un-fatherly question I've ever heard.

'Neither of us is the man. It doesn't work like that.' I say, embarrassed. I down a whole half of a glass of wine. 'It's not like that.'

'So how do you have sex?' he asks. 'You can tell me now.' He leans forward.

I don't believe this: now the preacher wants a sermon on lesbian sex. It is too much. You never expect to talk to your father about sex, any father, adoptive or birth, about any sex, heterosexual or lesbian. But he won't let the matter drop. He keeps on. He reaches into the depths of his imagination for one final image. 'So what do you do? You squeeze each other's titties and so on and so forth?'

'And the rest,' I say under my breath, sweating now. I look at the turquoise blue of the pool with some longing. I would love to run along the diving board and take a beautiful, breath-taking dive into the pool. Not a belly flap. Not a lesbian belly flap – a beautiful fish arc of a dive.

Jonathan seems to realise that he is not going to get more salacious details out of me. Strangely enough, though, he has not been at all judgemental in the way I'd feared. So that's something. Quite the opposite.

Red Dust Road by Jackie Kay (Picador, 2011)

THE POEMS

Darling

You might forget the exact sound of her voice,
Or how her face looked when sleeping.
You might forget the sound of her quiet weeping
Curled into the shape of a half moon,

When smaller than her self, she seemed already to be leaving
Before she left, when the blossom was on the trees
And the sun was out, and all seemed good in the world.
I held her hand and sang a song from when I was a girl –

Heil Ya Ho Boys, Let her go Boys
And when I stopped singing she had slipped away,
Already a slip of a girl again, skipping off,
Her heart light, her face almost smiling.

And what I didn't know, or couldn't see then,
Was that she hadn't really gone.
The dead don't go till you do, loved ones.
The dead are still here holding our hands.

'Darling' originally published in Jackie Kay's *Darling: New & Selected Poems* (Bloodaxe Books, 2007)

Here's My Pitch

Let Arthur Wharton come back from the dead
To see the man in black blow the final whistle.
Let the game of two halves be beautiful,
Not years ahead. Let every kissing of the badge,
Every cultured pass, every lad and lass,
Every uttered thought, every chant and rant,
Every strip and stripe – be free of it.

Then football would have truly played a blinder,
And Arthur returned to something kinder.
Let the man in black call time on racism.
And Arthur will sing out on the wings,
Our presiding spirit – the first black blade.
Imagine having everything to play for.
This is our pitch. Now hear us roar.

Arthur Wharton, half-Scottish, half-Grenadian, was the first black footballer to play professionally in the Football League, joining Sheffield United in 1894.

'Here's My Pitch' was published in the *Guardian* (26 October, 2012), the Friday after Jackie's visit to Styal; the RISE event was its first public reading. Jackie Kay later read the poem on the pitch of Sheffield United's Bramhall Lane as part of the 'kick it out' campaign. You can read more about Arthur Wharton and the Bramhall Lane reading on the *Guardian*'s webpage: http://www.guardian.co.uk/books/2012/oct/26/jackie-kay-poetry-football-racism

THE READING REVOLUTION

ATTEMPTS TO HELP

Grace Farrington

t is an interesting experiment to use the same poem with different groups. In the example given below, the same poem has been read in four different Get Into Reading groups, all of which are involved in Reader Organisation research projects. Two groups take place in community mental health settings, whereas the other two are based on in-patient wards for older people requiring acute psychiatric care. With the last two it has not been possible to audio record every session due to issues with obtaining consent from service users, but the project worker's diary serves as a record of what happened during each session, in the early stages of the group. In what follows the main detail is therefore taken from the transcript of one of the community group sessions, with comparisons being made in the course of it to other sessions.

The group meets in a public library in a small space at the back that has been adopted for the purpose. Advertised specifically to mental health service users living in the community, it has attracted people from a range of socio-economic and educational backgrounds. Now in its fourth month, there are several committed members, and others are continuing to join.

Along with the project worker and Jackie, the community mental health nurse who also assists with the running of the group, there are five people present today. Two tend to be very quiet: a visibly withdrawn lady whose husband brings her to the group and picks her up each week, and a man in his sixties who is always polite, yet difficult to connect with as a person. Then there are two women who had known each other before coming to the group: a recovered alcoholic who, as she says, has struggled with emotional problems, and a lady who, always arriving early to get herself settled before the group assembles, seems to rely on having control of her own space. Another woman, younger and with an open, friendly look about her, has been told about the group by her social worker, and joins us for the first time.

In the novel that the group are reading, the father of the protagonist, whose story the book has been tracing from his early childhood, has just died of cancer, not long after the protagonist's quickly arranged wedding. The poem 'Comfort' by Elizabeth Jennings is chosen to follow this, perhaps to collect some of the emotion that the narrative has raised which by its very nature cannot be resolved, at least at this point.

> **Hand closed upon another, warm.**
> **The other, cold, turned round and met**
> **And found a weather made of calm.**
> **So sadness goes, and so regret.**
>
> **A touch, a magic in the hand.**
> **Not what the fortune-teller sees**
> **Or thinks that she can understand.**
> **This warm hand binds but also frees.**

Following the reading there is a pause before the project worker asks if anyone has anything they would like to say about the poem.

> *Richard*: **Well I don't really understand it at first.**
> *Amanda*: **I was thinking the same. I'm glad you said that.**
> *Jackie*: **I tell you what I didn't understand. The first bit: 'The other, cold, turned around, and met / and found a weather made of calm.'**
> *Project worker*: **Lines 2 and 3.**

At present the project worker is simply glad that the group is starting to get over the hurdle of not understanding. To first acknowledge this hurdle is an often necessary step before what we call 'getting into' the poem. A certain level of difficulty in the poem is useful too though, in that it makes the members of a group necessary to one another. There would be less to be gained if everyone understood individually straightaway.

> *Gill*: **Well that's the one that's receiving the hand. The one that needs comfort.**
> *Richard*: **Is it just a stranger he's met though? They're shaking hands.**
> *Cathy*: **Something might have happened, so they're giving the hand to help you, you know to comfort you.**

Gill has helped with her instinctive understanding of what is going on in the poem. She has often seemed particularly alert to what in her words would be the emotional difficulty found expressed in poems. Her use of a vocabulary adjacent to that of the poem – 'receiving' – has also prompted Cathy in her answer about 'giving'. The paired patterning of the poem is being adhered to: met and found, binding but freeing. And this is where Cathy tends to be strongest, in her ability to come in and build upon what someone else has said.

There is something to be said in response to Richard about the way in which the poem holds his own idea alongside that offered by Cathy. The effect of the strangeness of one person to another is not removed by the meeting point between them, and yet the meeting is a means of comfort. But there will be time to approach this in a less abstract way once the group are firmly *in* the poem.

Aware that Richard in particular seems still to be feeling as if he were somewhat on the outside, the project worker goes back and reads the poem a second time.

> *Richard*: **Is he at a fortune teller's?**
> *Jackie*: **I suppose you do give them your hand don't you.**
> *Project worker*: **Literally, yes. It's strange that mention of the fortune-teller in line 6 though isn't it. I mean it doesn't sound like any words are exchanged.**
> *Amanda*: **'A touch, a magic in the hand.' Just the physical touch is comforting isn't it. Just the sheer warmth of somebody...**

Project worker: **Yes, 'this warm hand'.**

Richard: **Maybe that second verse is saying you know the fortune-teller doesn't realise the power that she's actually got. And how important just a touch is. Cause she has loads of hands put in front of her. It's just work for her.**

Richard begins to see a way in which the poem might hold meaning for him. He is taking it too literally of course – since the fortune-teller is used negatively, as an analogy suggestive of the attempt to understand another person. It is the fortune-teller that the poem is actually trying to get away from. But the project worker is loath simply to correct Richard. He is getting somewhere imaginatively even within his mistake. Reimagining 'the fortune-teller' as a character embodied within the poem, Richard is able to guess at the feeling involved, both for the professional – 'it's just work' – and the person on the receiving end. He adds in front of those phrases offered by the new group member, Amanda – 'just the touch' / 'just the sheer warmth': '*how important* just a touch is'. He is still not quite understanding the poem on its own terms, but misreadings are something that reader-outreach projects have to work upon. In three out of the four groups, interest has gathered around this figure of the fortune-teller, perhaps in view of the lack of literal things – nouns and named persons – in the poem for the reader to fix their attention upon. Less experienced readers, particularly of poetry, often seem to find it harder to get beyond the literal.

The two verses having each been looked at separately, the project worker feels that a final opportunity to respond to the poem as a whole will help the group. Richard, feeling more engaged by the poem, opts to read some of it, taking the first verse. The project worker reads the second. Joan then speaks up – although with the library having reopened after its hour-long close, the atmosphere of concentration in the group is beginning to break down.

Joan: **I think it's trying to say that sometimes you don't need any words to be spoken do you and if you, you know just a touch onto somebody...**

Jackie: [having been distracted by library staff] **What was that Joan, what did you say there? We missed that.**
Joan: **I know. I don't know it's sort of like trying to say that you don't need any words to say** [phone rings, interrupting] **See I'm not meant to say anything.**
Gill: **Third time lucky Joan!**
Jackie: **Go on Joan.**
Joan: **No, I'm done now.**

Having taken a risk in putting herself forward, Joan finds herself without the support of those whose role it is to help the group, and making her point becomes harder than anticipated. It is not uncommon for such statements, tentatively made in approaching breakthrough, to get missed by a project worker, whose attention is occupied also with the need to manage group events. But there is a cost to missing them: not only is the breakthrough lost but the new level of confidence that the person is stepping into is potentially curbed.

Joan feels strongly about this idea of not always needing verbal communication, which she has tried repeatedly to put forward.

Since her referral to Mersey Care services a couple of years back, which had led to her dual diagnosis of depression and personality disorder, Joan has been through a long course of counselling, becoming familiar as a result with the kinds of language used in therapy. The project worker has been told that she has been resistant to counselling, feeling patronised, and her behaviour suggests that she values the group for the ways in which it contrasts with talking therapy. Whilst both Jackie and the social worker who attends make attempts at times to engage the group, Joan is often reluctant to answer questions posed directly to her, and rarely talks about herself. She is more likely, as in the present example, to volunteer a response to the text on instinct, without the help of a facilitator's intervention.

In the notes about her experience of the group which Joan later shows the project worker (in an effort to help with the research), she describes having been 'quite defensive' in relation to the psychological support that she receives, as when a member of the mental health team rings to arrange to cover her regular appointment with the support worker who is on leave. Joan may have developed a trust of individuals, such as the support worker whom she always refers to simply by first name, but she does not necessarily trust either the system or the method of treatment. In fact, the week after the group had been reading 'Comfort', Jackie reported that Joan had stated to the service her upset and anger regarding aspects of the treatment she had been receiving, and that the only positive comment she had made had been about the reading group. Three months later, after a visit to the doctor which had left her feeling 'preoccupied and a little down', Joan would describe the 'tonic' of being able to come to the group and, rather than relay all her problems, spend time in the company of other people, listening.

Of the texts that the group have read, one of Joan's favourites is 'The Door' by Helen Simpson. The story features two characters: a bereaved woman who for some months has remained isolated in her grief, and a man from the local DIY shop who arrives to fit her new door. The woman expects nothing but irritation from the visit, and yet the man's manner proves to be in every way opposite to what she had feared. His smile is 'unforced' and 'natural'. The following two sentences indicate the woman's relief:

> **He was not going to be chatty, how wonderful; I would be able to trust him and leave him to it and get on with my work... There was satisfaction in two people working separately but companionably in the flat. It was dignified.**

Joan liked this passage. Both the story and the poem 'Comfort' share this sense of the *dignity* of being allowed to be side to side, no one person intruding on the other.

Something of this theme is apparent as Joan is urged by the others to repeat herself once more.

> *Joan*: **Sometimes you know if somebody's worried about something you don't need to say any words do you, you know you just need to go** [places her hand on Gill]
> *Cathy*: **Touch of the hand.**

> *Joan*: **Yeah and that's comfort in itself. And the person who's giving you the comfort they're not saying 'I understand how you feel' or, or anything like that. Cause it says the fortune-teller – he's not trying to say 'I know how you feel'. They just want you to know that**
> *Cathy*: [reaching out to touch Joan] **They're there.**
> *Joan*: **so somebody's there yeah for you.**
> *Jackie*: **Like in a friendship.**

The responses here, both verbal and non-verbal, engage the whole person. These people are responding to the poem and to each other, and working together now, a bit like the parts of a poem, or a group of musicians. Cathy, despite her characteristic quietness, has stepped up her response to Joan, having seen the opening and the need. Her fillers, by supplying just the final portion of the sentence: a noun phrase ('Touch of the hand') and a short clause ('[to know that] they're there'), help to make sure that what was thwarted earlier will reach a completion, not by interrupting but adding in where a space has been left. She does it without straying from the poem's use of the third person. It is not 'I'm here' or 'we're here' that she adds but 'They're there'.

Even so, Joan's unfinished formulation 'They just want you to know that...' is probably (thinks the project worker, later) the best account of the unspokenness in the poem. It would be better for this to have been left as it was without Jackie's closing and normalising explanation.

Joan's complaint has been in regard to people who, seeking to give comfort, take on an overly familiar manner towards the other person. Their phrasing may be well-meaning but it is almost too *appropriate*, too easily stated: 'I understand; I know how you feel'. The poem, on the other hand, holds back from any such confident 'saying'. In Joan's paraphrase, the previous order of the pronouns is reversed. 'I know how you...' becomes, in a shift of emphasis from 'I' to 'you', 'They want you to know...' A different type of knowing is suggested, which, along with the poem, 'also frees', leaving space for the other person.

A member of the other community group recognises that such restraint is represented also within the form of the poem:

Simon: **It's such a short poem, it says it without having too many superfluous words doesn't it. So it's very powerful for such a concise poem.**

But there is something else you might have noticed in the transcript above: Joan touching Gill, Cathy touching Joan. In this physical acting out of the poem it is as though the language has been answered by the corresponding behaviour: a touch, which in turn recreates the impression of the poem as it were in the flesh.

In the example of Angela, a member of one of the inpatient groups, the potential for the effect of the poem to be lasting is even more evident. Angela kept her copy of 'Comfort' and for several months after we had read it together would occasionally make reference to how it had stuck with her. Angela suffers from a severe mental illness, with symptoms of psychosis and very low mood, and yet is able to maintain a level of functioning and clarity of mind at times that many of the other patients on the ward do not have.

On one occasion she admitted how difficult this could be for her. Speaking, once the session had finished, about the failure of her attempts when sitting in the lounge to talk to other patients, and to get a response from them, she commented, 'I think they think I'm looking at them.' In the poem, however, such silence and the sense of isolation that comes with it seems to be abated for Angela.

Angela: **There's a lovely one I like. 'Comfort' I think. It's the most loveliest piece of poetry I've ever come across. Very loving it is. It built me.**

That the poem is both 'lovely' and even 'loving' suggests its value as a document of human feeling; almost like a person as it were who becomes touchingly present in the reading of it. Where human interaction is missing, and missed, the poem seems to be able to provide a genuine, sustaining form of comfort. 'It built me' is an extraordinary formulation: a language response exceeding normal expression and itself a tribute to poetry.

POETRY

MICHAEL O'NEILL

Belief

He burned to believe as a child
　　in Father Christmas and God.
The former's fate and they chuckled;
　　with the latter's abscondment something had faltered.

Young, he credited little,
　　believing a theme best postponed.
He'd not have it sorted; he'd gobble
　　the fruit, then examine the rind.

A middle-aged man, he'd sit in a church,
　　and do so not solely for bust or for Titian.
To capture how longings might differ or match
　　over years had emerged as his mission.

Older, at night, it seemed harder to breathe;
　　pains added up to a composite ache
as if saying, 'Writhe
　　and suffer, sir sceptic; a wreck

of yourself as you were, imagine how worse
　　it'll get between now and the end;
meditate, brood and rehearse;
　　give thought to your end.'

But what to do with this voice in a dream:
　　What we know is the ash; what we hope
for's the fire; knowing may be a sham,
　　hope means we can leap?

Intimates

I took my illness to Valladolid;
it didn't do much there; it merely hid
among the tapas, Castile stone, and laughter,
the visits to the Plaza late at night.

My illness and myself became good friends;
we knew the road ahead had hidden bends,
but tramped in close communion round Wastwater,
not letting one another out of sight.

We found our way to Venice, worries now
bravely laid aside, ready to allow
for alterations – richer maybe, maybe poorer –
to rise from all that water, sun and light.

Severance at times was clearly on the cards;
San Marco in the evening pressed us hard.
The drawn-out small hours, though, brought us together,
hinting through shutters at a common plight.

Soulmates, we studied Ezra's church,
the 'jewel box' – when waves slapped, felt a lurch
in the heart, brain, viscera
at what remains and what is taking flight

in each ripple of the stream of moments
it all seems to come down to, a tense
that coalesces present, past and future,
in which we'll stage a scene of fright and fight.

Towards Sixty

you start to see
you had not been able to see
from any position
other than your own.

It had all been slightly
askew, the angle too tightly
found and secured,
the integrity immured.

Nor was there any getting out
of it, however you set about
amending it; you were stuck,
at the mercy of luck,

which might take pity,
offer you a different city,
say, but only to take your luggage
to, your scuffed baggage.

To be aware and alive
from one perspective!
For energy to dwell
in a locked cell!

Make do, you tell yourself;
no one's more than the single self.
Accept, provide, shut down;
assume a smile that's like a frown,

even if a better scribe
would seek to describe
a world elsewhere
with its need for prayer.

PHOTO ESSAY

UNDERGROUND NEW YORK PUBLIC LIBRARY

Sarah Coley browses the web

The Underground New York Public Library, a website created and kept up with friendly regularity by photographer Ourit Ben-Haim, has become an essential part of my internet browsing. The site offers a photographic series of NYC subway travellers with their books, a library on the move, together with internet links so that browsers can get hold of the book there and then, if tempted.

Below; *Blueberries for Sal*, Robert McCloskey

65

Above; *In Search of Lost Time*, Marcel Proust
Right; *Steve Jobs*, Walter Isaacson

'It's about to be a full year that I've been blogging the Underground Library. It's been a year of many discoveries and experiences. One discovery I had may seem plain but it felt profound to experience it through photography. I discovered that a reader is… a Reader. In looking for people who were reading, I found that they were there as a kind. Books weren't just an item they had with them. They were indications of a larger relationship that defined them. When I posted a reader whom I had photographed twice, someone commented that it was like a love story. I like that and I agree. Readers are in love with the world around them, and their relationship with the books that reveal it to them is an enduring one.'

– Ourit Ben-Haim

'I'm conscious of the rules but I break them if the moment calls for it. Street Photography is an uncontrolled endeavor, especially underground, on moving trains, crowded platforms, and barely lit subways. My efforts are always towards producing high quality images. My priority though is to capture a glimpse of us, even if it means some image noise, blown pixels, or an unexpected visual ratio. '

– Ourit Ben-Haim

page 68-9; *The Gift of Asher Lev,* Chaim Potok
Above; she's reading *Veinte poemas de amor y una cancion de desesperada y cien sonetos de amor,* Pablo Neruda; he's reading *Time Travel and Warp Drives: A Scientific Guide to Shortcuts through Time and Space,* Allen Everett and Thomas Roman

In a curious way, the mix of outward and inward dimensions in the photographs reminds me of the experience of watching sport – the involuntary focused way you're on the side of the player, feeling it in your own arms and legs (as a child I was always the horse at the Horse of the Year Show), as if what the reader or the sportsperson is doing does *you* good. We can all be defensively separate from our fellow travellers but the book doesn't seem isolating in the same way that the smartphone or the mp3 player are (though no doubt a private solace to the reader). Is reading communal somehow even when silent and apart? I will continue to haunt Ourit's site and hope one day to spy our Enid there.

All photographs by Ourit Ben-Haim, with many thanks.
http://undergroundnewyorkpubliclibrary.com

THE READING REVOLUTION

ON READING ALOUD

Veronika Carnaby

I remember my grammar school days in near vivid detail – clutching my mother's coat in trepidation while waiting for the front entrance gates to open, taking my wooden classroom bench in solitude, hands clasped and isolated in a cocoon of silence. It was remarkable how lonely I felt amidst the hustle and bustle of a New York City public school. I wasn't punished nor was I a shy youngster but rather a pensive one. I simply refused to engage in conversation with anyone aside from my closest mates – not even the teachers. 'How are we doing today, Veronika?' Ms. Zinnia, my teacher would ask me. 'Did you have any problems with last night's workbook exercises?' I shook my head from side to side. It would take a lot more than that to coax my voice out. I focused my gaze on the floor or down my pleated uniform skirt until her attention shifted elsewhere.

Were it not for my love of language arts, I would have found myself in a complete state of misery. But to my great good fortune, I found my calling early on and looked forward to our daily spelling tests, phonics work, and most of all, reading periods. I'd check out a mountainous stack of books from the library the prior evening, stuff the load in my knapsack, and unzip it over my school desk the next day, only to be drowned in a sea of literature from Carroll, Hughes, and London. Then I'd pack them up, walk home, and back to the library to start all over again. My folks nurtured this passion of mine and often encouraged me to approach Ms. Zinnia and read her a few words from one of my books in the hope that I'd open up – an offer I never really thought I'd take up until that fateful Thursday afternoon when I emerged from the shadows.

While all the kids had obediently lined up in a single file, backpacks strapped on and coats buttoned up, waiting for their parents to collect them, I paced back and forth waiting for the right time to strike with what I felt was a tremendous act of bravery on my part. When the coast was clear, I gave Ms. Zinnia a tap on the back, flipped open my tattered paperback *Alice's Adventures in Wonderland*, and read sentences, paragraphs, pages out loud. By the time I finished, a rush of adrenaline had claimed me. She knelt beside me, looked me square in the eye and said, 'I knew you had it in you. I'm proud of you, really!'

My world changed from that point on. I brought in a new story to slug through with her the next day, next week, and next month, and eventually found myself comfortable enough to forge a lasting relationship with her, my instructor, of all people. Before long, reading aloud became my second nature and my classmates, a second family. I unknowingly become a part of a greater community.

With time, I longed to pass the torch and change the life of another young kid like my former self, so I took up a tutoring stint to guide students through reading books out loud. I had the pleasure of working with an Indian fellow named Sajeev, bowl haircut, telling doe eyes, quiet as can be, ashamed of his speech impediment. 'Coo you, woo you?' he whispered and scanned the room for any prying souls who might deflate his troubled confidence. I pushed him, 'Say it louder kid, with all your might! Read it with the soul and energy that bubbles within you. Could, coo, would, woo, it makes no difference, so long as you read it with passion. We're not here to judge.' He took that advice and ran like Seabiscuit on the racetrack, devouring his greatest foe, and reveling in the collective support.

But somewhere along the way, the innocence faded. The practice of vocal reading suddenly went out of style, put on the backburner like some leftover stew. I seized any opportunity I could to utter the sweet sound of words, and not just in books.

During my frequent travels around the country, I read every road sign I laid my eyes on: 'Reduce speed, jughandle ahead. Better watch out, it says that stopping and standing is prohibited at any time and that violators'll be towed.' When writing sparked my interest, I never deemed a poem finished until I read and re-read each stanza at least twice. Call it mad, call it eccentric, but for me, it was just plain the way I functioned. Others who shared my affinity were few and far between, and I vowed to confront someone, anyone about this thing that had now become a faint recollection to most.

I spotted Victor, a distant friend of mine, leaning against a railing with an open book and a fervent expression. 'Say Vic,' I asked after some five minutes, 'why do you prefer reading to yourself?'

'It's faster,' he answered. 'I can just scan the words and get on with it. The question is why waste time reading every single word out loud?'

I told him, 'It's not just about reading the words. It's about saying them and feeling them, *being* them. They leap off the page, you see, straight from the writer's heart to yours, and you bring everyone along for the ride. Kinda like a song. It looks great on paper, but the magic comes to life when it's sung.' He said nothing, glazed his eyes back over at his book, furrowed his brows, and carried on.

Years later, I came to realize that there was much more to reading aloud than I had previously thought. On a black November evening, I gathered with my pals at a smoky, underground club in the heart of Boston, Massachusetts, famous for its open mic nights. Anyone was free to take the stage and perform whatever they pleased, be it poetry or those jazzy rock 'n roll tunes that everyone loved so much. That particular evening, someone handed me and the rest of my company a copy of Jack Kerouac's *On the Road* and began reciting some passages. Though I'd read the work in all its brilliance in the past, I fell in love with it all over again. I felt caught in an otherworldly experience hearing it voiced, assuming the role of Sal and Dean in their vagrant adventures; everything played out before me and I found myself in their shoes. But the biggest kick of all was the sense of togetherness in the club. I wasn't alone in riding Kerouac's rollercoaster. All twenty of us stashed our differences aside – age, race, beliefs, past – to be transported. To be one.

'Man, can you believe those guys?' Kenny, the painfully shyest of the bunch, yelped from across the room. 'I would kill to be a fly on the wall of their '49 Hudson.'

'Right, right,' everyone agreed with lingering astonishment at Kenny's sudden outspokenness.

In the dead of the night when even the moon slept under cloudy covers, I rushed home to lend an ear to Allen Ginsberg's recorded public *HOWL* reading, a powerful and inspirational poetic performance. Boy, that did it. Well into his reading, I envisioned the entire San Francisco gathered round the foot of his chair, gaping at his spectacled face, eagerly awaiting the next remark from his babbling mouth. In my head, I saw audience and reader joining forces and experiencing life as an entity rather than as unsolved puzzle pieces, and that's when it struck me: reading out loud was more than just an essence, more than an audible sensation. It was a reminder of camaraderie, of a human spirit bound since the days of yore, one which prevailed through joy and bereavement alike to be celebrated at public gatherings like this.

Today when others ask me 'Why read out loud?' I simply reply, 'Why not?' When people dare to vocally embrace the language, to read it, shout it, sing it, mush it between their teeth and tongues, they rally with the writer and with those around them. They stand united as a whole. They tune into unspoken thoughts, give a voice to the voiceless, and even extend a loving hand to those that share the experience. So I say, read on before others. Join a group. Share some words with a loved one or two. Dare to speak out. After all, what is there to lose when you gain a community?

YOUR REGULARS

C-A-R-R-O-T-S

Ian McMillan

This is a story about reading, and about hope. It's about hope dashed and then rekindled. It's about travel, and going to a place far away. But it's mainly about reading.

It was the Easter Holidays sometime in the mid-1960s; Easter must have been late that year because the holiday days were warm and I was spending a lot of time between my Auntie's on North Street and my mates Geoff and Keith and Robert and Stuart, and the little library in the village. I must have been eight, maybe, or nine.

I'd been getting lots of books out of the library with clever animals in them. You know the kind of thing: dogs who save entire families from barn fires; parrots who shout to alert slumbering shopkeepers of the robber's arrival; pigeons who brave the horrors of war to deliver news from the soldiers at the front to the officers at the back.

Mrs. Beck, who lived next door to my auntie, had a cat. I can't recall the name of the cat but Mrs. Beck said it was, in her words, 'as clever as a schoolteacher'. She'd look over her fence at us and say 'It knows every word you say, you know.' The cat would gaze at her with an air of detached feline cynicism and Mrs Beck would say 'Do you want some tea?' and the cat would wag its tail and Mrs Beck would grin triumphantly and repeat her catchphrase. 'Clever as a schoolteacher.'

Geoff said we should try out the cat with a few unfamiliar words. 'Let's say 'umbrella' to it and see what happens' he said, and we nodded. But we never got round to it. It was that kind of holiday.

That night, I thought about the clever cat. I thought about the animals that saved people in the books I read from the library. I thought about our pet, the lethargic rabbit Bunny Fluff, a huge white presence that just sat around in its hutch waiting for the next lettuce leaf, and I tried to imagine Bunny Fluff starring in an adventure where it jumped into a runaway car and somehow managed to press the brakes with its ears, saving some triplets from serious and lasting injury.

I fell asleep and had an odd dream and in the dream Bunny Fluff was not only doing amazing things that were written about in books, he was reading the books, too. In the dream he wore a pair of outsize glasses like Brains had in *Thunderbirds*. In the dream he read the books avidly and towards the end of the dream, as I was waking up, he took them back to the library to get some more.

I woke up and said, aloud, to the empty room 'I'm going to teach Bunny Fluff to read!' That became my mission that year, as Easter melted into late Spring and Summer came in through the open window. I'd sit in front of Bunny Fluff's cage with an old *Mac and Tosh* book from school and I'd try to teach the rabbit what the words meant, which was what I understood reading to be. I'd hold the book very close to BF's pink eyes and then I'd say the words slowly. This is Mac. This is Tosh. See Mac. See Tosh. Maybe I should have started with a higher species like Mrs. Beck's cat. Maybe I should have taken notice of the lads when they asked me why I thought Bunny Fluff would read in English. This is Mac. I see Mac. Do you see Mac?

Keith announced that he was moving to Australia with his family. Actually, announced is too strong a word. He just said it, one afternoon as we were pouring a bucket of water on some ants. There was a pause, a gap in the conversation. 'They'll have big ants in Australia' Geoff said, 'Big as Mrs. Beck's cat'. 'I'll be able to teach them to read' Keith laughed, and I punched him.

But, why not? Why couldn't animals (and birds, and fish if you could develop a waterproof book) learn to read? I loved reading, and I'd attempted to teach my Uncle Charlie to read and because I was on the top table at school I'd sat with some of the kids on the bottom table to help them with their reading. Everybody should read. Every living creature.

Keith and his family eventually went to Australia just before the six-week holidays in July. One day he was there and the next day there was an empty place in the school dinner queue. We were, I guess, sad for a while but then we put him to the back of our minds and gazed at the empty vista of the summer.

I carried on with Bunny Fluff. I decided he wasn't making any progress because he thought Mac and Tosh were boring so I read him comics, *The Beano* and *The Dandy*. Still very slowly, still very close to his eyes. I thought he liked Alf Tupper best, but that could well have been just my imagination.

Then, at the end of August, I got a letter from Keith. It wasn't a very interesting letter, to be honest; it just said they'd got there okay and his dad had got a job and there was a lad from Rotherham in the class called Derek. At the end he put a PS: 'Are you still trying to get that rabbit to read? Well, read him this letter.'

And I did. And I'm sure I saw his eyes following the words as I held the paper up. I'm sure I saw his eyes undulating with something like comprehension.

THE READING REVOLUTION

THE MOOKSE AND THE GRIPES

Dennis Walder

Some years ago I was responsible for compiling a booklet of Supplementary Texts for use by students and tutors at Open University Literature Summer Schools formerly held at the University of York. Creating such a booklet was a mind-bending exercise, despite the assistance of experienced colleagues, since the critical extracts, prose and poetry in the sixty-page booklet formed the basis of intensive work during each week of tutorials, seminars and lectures. Students also used course set texts and other material, but the supplementary booklet had to provide for lively, relevant and worthwhile sessions every week for several weeks over the years of a course life.

One of the sessions was on Modernism, and in addition to such familiar voices as those of Joseph Conrad, T.S. Eliot and Virginia Woolf, I wished to include something by James Joyce – and particularly something from his most radical excursion into 'making it new', *Finnegans Wake* (1939). Joyce spent seventeen years writing this work, probably his least read, yet most experimental.

My task was made easier by the fact that I had myself not had the stamina to pursue every last word of this astonishing, multilingual text, drawn from over sixty world languages, although predominantly in English, and filled with puns, portmanteau words and phrases so as to carry several layers of meaning at once. I couldn't claim to understand every word of the extract I decided upon; but at least, I said to myself, it offered a kind of story, and was, as far as I could tell, comic.

'Eins within a space and a wearywide space it wast ere wohned a Mookse', my 30-line extract began, echoing a traditional story opening, but with a strangely Germanic ring – aptly enough, I realised, given the Germanic roots of so many stories of friendly animals such as, I supposed, a 'mookse' – which, like the fox of Aesop's famous fable, spurns the grapes he cannot reach because, he claims, they are sour. But it was only when I heard myself saying 'gripes' that I realised I was saying 'grapes' with a joke-German accent, and indeed that as I enunciated the rest of the text, it was full of signals suggesting jokey accents and even a dreamily sing-song voice, helping me to understand what was going on in this night-time text (Joyce himself called the *Wake* a night book, complementing the single day of *Ulysses*).

I had never before tried reading the text aloud. But it was thanks to the fact that, in order to make the booklet more easily available to our blind or partially-sighted students, several of us (including the then Vice-Chancellor's wife) recorded the extracts on tape. Joyce himself had poor eyesight, and was nearly blind by the time he finished the work. And it was only when recording myself reading it out loud that I discovered how much easier it was to understand than on the page when, typically, our eyes speed over the lines far too quickly to comprehend something as gloriously multiplicitous and suggestive as the *Wake*.

POETRY

THE OLD POEM

Brian Nellist

Fulke Greville, Lord Brooke (1554–1628)
'Caelica' (1633), 100.

In night when colours all to black are cast,
Distinction lost, or gone down with the light;
The eye a watch to inward senses plac'd,
Not seeing, yet still having power of sight,

Gives vain alarums to the inward sense,
Where fear stirr'd up with witty tyranny,
Confounds all powers, and thorough self-offence,
Doth forge and raise impossibility:

Such as in thick depriving darknesses,
Proper reflections of the error be,
And images of self-confusednesses,
Which hurt imaginations only see;
    And from this nothing seen, tells news of devils,
    Which but expressions be of inward evils.

ON 'CAELICA'

Famously, Greville summarised his life in his epitaph, 'Servant to Queen Elizabeth, Councillor to King James, Friend to Sir Philip Sidney', as though that final relationship mattered most, as it did for his poetry. Yet his verse differs greatly, more austere, less warm and sprightly than his friend's. His sonnets address Myra and Caelica but they are almost aspects of his own feelings, the former more physical and the latter more of the mind. If that seems chilling compared with the dramatic presence of Stella in Sidney's sequence, Greville's poems are consistently more philosophical, as here. That wonderfully spare line four, 'Not seeing, yet still having power of sight,' seems at first an invitation to fantasy of which the whole poem is, however, dismissive, an 'impossibility' (8). What he sees instead is the work of the moral sense, of guilt or, to use the language so severe a Calvinist would use, of sin. Imagination becomes a 'witty tyranny', the noun dismissive of the work of 'wit', the rational mind. Twice he uses instead the word 'self'; he is overthrown through 'self-offence', the self-harm of excessive guilt. There is no elegance in this poetry but instead a knotted and blinding honesty which, granting all the differences of assumption, reminds me of Hardy. 'Self-confusednesses', for example, has a comparable clumsy economy, in which confusion is both source and product of the state of mind in which nightmare mingles with waking fears. 'Hurt imaginations is still better in its ambiguous adjective, both subject to an inflicted wound but also to inherent disability. This is a sonnet on the English model where everything depends on the final couplet, as its critics claim. But after all the waywardness of seeing and not seeing, there is a resolved dismissal of the fantastic language of devils for what are truly expressions... 'of inward evils', within his competence under God. There was a good modernised edition by Thom Gunn of the whole sequence published by Faber. Read 'O wearisome condition of humanity' from his drama *Mustapha* alongside *King Lear*.

THE READING REVOLUTION

THE OTHER SIDE OF EXPERIENCE

Casi Dylan

We had had to haggle with the taxi driver at Ajloun. We didn't want the short ride back and forth to the fort like the other travellers, but a longer drive up through the Jordan Valley to Pella, and our next room for the night. (Later, from Pella, we would take the bus to the ancient site of Gadara and, sitting with legs hanging from a rock on the town's high periphery, take in Israel, the Golan Heights, Syria, the Sea of Galilee.) Now the fare was finally settled, I got into the back and leaned my head against the clouded window. The car climbed out of town. Back on track. We'd been looking forward to the adventure of Pella.

It took me by surprise, as we broke the crest of a hill and for the first time saw the full expanse of the valley, to find tears in my eyes. It was beautiful; and yet it wasn't beauty alone which had moved me. It was something less expected than that, a kind of recognition. Because whilst here I was in unknown northern Jordan, there was something in the incline of the hillside, or the depth at which the river flowed, or the scene's sudden greenness that brought Cwmystwyth home to me. The drive up to Cwmystwyth from Devil's Bridge, the road which had time and again led me back to my small white childhood home. And I was there, and I was here in Jordan in the back of this car, and I can't work out why this strange familiarity has brought the tears to my eyes. Later on in that trip Robin tells me that I, turning to him in my half-sleep, spoke to him in Welsh. 'It must be all these places we've been going to', I say. 'I've known them all from years back. Sunday school.' Twenty years ago now. *Canaan. Jiwdea. Nebo. Môr Galilea.*

*

Months later and I'm back in Scotland – Edinburgh Central Library – and there are eight of us round the table reading Wordsworth. It's a masterclass called 'The Consequences of Beauty', and we begin with 'Lines Written a Few Miles Above Tintern Abbey'. As might be expected when a name and reputation such as Wordsworth's is involved, there is some apprehension in the room about diving in. We read the poem aloud in its entirety twice – wonderful! wonderful! – and some of these anxieties come out straight away: mostly they relate to the length of the piece – 'You could never fit it into just one session!' – its density, tone, some educational hangovers. These are nothing that building a reading stamina of your own can't tackle, and surely this is what masterclasses are for: to remind facilitators that behind the basic practices of shared reading there remains that fundamental need to keep on reading for your own personal meaning, ungoverned by the specific requirements of such-and-such a setting, such-and-such a time limit. Always go back, begin with the bits that move you. Here is one of mine, early on in the poem in which the Wye valley's 'forms of beauty' are felt to have inspired:

> **sensations sweet,**
> **Felt in the blood, and felt along the heart,**
> **And passing even into my purer mind**
> **With tranquil restoration: – feelings too**
> **Of unremembered pleasure; such, perhaps**
> **As may have had no trivial influence**
> **On that best portion of a good man's life;**
> **His little, nameless, unremembered acts**
> **Of kindness and of love.**

There is an important something in this passage for me – the repeated 'unremembered' perhaps? – connecting it somehow to that earlier drive in Jordan, and also with the practice of shared reading itself. Because surely this is the working faith of the facilitator, that those 'little, nameless' perhaps even 'unremembered' acts of shared meaning-making can be restored in and to a future as yet unknown. That through the deliberately untargeted structure of a session come 'pleasing thoughts / That in this moment there is life and food / For future years.' This is why we read in schools, with looked after children, with babies and their parents: the action is a pre-emptive statement of value. I think this is why 'no trivial influence' is a better claim than if the poem said 'great influence'. The tentative phrasing is a sign of a freedom that maybe makes change possible.

It so happened that another member of the group had also made a mark next to this passage in the margin, but for a different reason. 'Yes, that bit stood out to me too: "*That best portion of a good man's life*". Am I not right to call him smug here?' And this is where my anxieties kick in. Fear that the strength of my feeling for this poem inversely limits my ability to do my job, to lead this session in a balanced way. I cannot hear comments about smugness, snobbery, irrelevance – and yet I know that it is a facilitator's job to listen. I cannot accept ready-made thoughts on this poem, but, surely – I hear the counter-argument – isn't it the facilitator's job to be prepared?

In that session I had to make a resolution to teach. If there is one piece of advice that we give more often than any other on Read to Lead, it is to remind facilitators to hold back on giving answers, reverting to 'teacher-mode'. Leading a shared reading group is different, freer than a classroom environment: the facilitators who do this well are those who can balance the necessary involvement and distance that best serves the group. And yet, the more I develop in this work, the more I understand that to cling to neutrality at all costs does a disservice both to the literature and to the group. And it is especially important to see that here – in a masterclass – where we have come together in consciousness of the need to improve our practice. Stepping up to teach in this setting did not make me the 'master' but rather drew necessary attention to Wordsworth's mastery: what I had to teach in that session was to show what it is like to be *able to learn*. This is especially pertinent in the case of Wordsworth, in which modes of learning and a certain kind of 'preparation' are at the heart of what he writes. From the very beginning of our session, in both of those initial readings, the word that stood out to us above all others was 'again', 'again', 'again'. Crucially, we're beginning with a return to Tintern Abbey following a gap of 'five summers, with the length / Of five long winters!'

**Once again
Do I behold these steep and lofty cliffs,
Which in a wild secluded scene impress
Thoughts of more deep seclusion; and connect
The landscape with the quiet of the sky.**

The scene is particular, 'these' cliffs are well-known and well-loved, but there's a wonderful 'more' to it all, even at this early stage of the poem, which connects not only the 'landscape with the quiet of the sky' but to those 'thoughts', themselves both deep secluded and 'impressed'. It's this active intermingling of directions and influences that runs through the whole piece, a mingling that must be familiar to anyone who's participated in a shared reading group. In Read to Lead we present the shared reading dynamic as a balancing of three main factors – Book, Individual, Group – each of which should overlap to form a cohesive, unique experience:

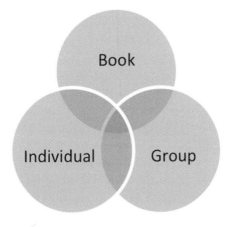

It's neat and useful on the page, but in reality how simplified it is, inadequate. The model in real life is as complex and powerful as a poem, and 'something far more deeply interfused'.

Roisin still prefers Lord Byron. I had brought along a passage from *Manfred* to read as a counterpoint to 'Tintern Abbey'. Here is Manfred at the beginning of Act II, standing at the edge of a precipice:

> **Beautiful!**
> **How beautiful is all this visible world!**
> **How glorious in its action and itself;**
> **But we, who name ourselves its sovereigns, we,**
> **Half dust, half deity, alike unfit**
> **To sink or soar, with our mixed essence make**
> **A conflict of its elements, and breathe**
> **The breath of degradation and of pride,**
> **Contending with low wants and lofty will**
> **Till our mortality predominates,**
> **And men are – what they name not to themselves,**
> **And trust not to each other.**

'*This* is real', says Roisin. 'This is what it is like.' And of course she is right. To be incapacitated by virtue of what we are, stuck, mixed, 'alike unfit / To sink or soar' is real, and painful, and more immediately recognisable than someone 'passing even into my purer mind / With tranquil restoration'. It can be infuriating to hear Wordsworth speak as if from the other side of an experience, one which is not necessarily ours. It is the song of a man who has come through. But if we are to be part of a reading revolution that works for the practical benefits of great literature, then we need to believe that this experience *could* be ours, or at least that it is somehow connected to it. We must expect that there can be 'more' and name it to ourselves, and trust it to each other. Here, where Manfred cannot speak, Wordsworth offers 'love' and 'kindness' and 'moral' and 'pleasure' and 'my dearest Friend, / My dear, dear Friend'. For all of Manfred's repeated 'we' there is no such togetherness.

I remember when I first read Wordsworth the electric shock of what I have now come to understand as recognition of a certain way of seeing the world. For a long time I did not know what to do with this. Perhaps I still don't, but I cannot think of a better practical expression of it than working with shared reading, of learning alongside others about how it works, what it can do, and how to recognise its particular qualities. And what I find best of all is that even within 'Tintern Abbey's' unique and powerful vision is the clear acknowledgment of distance travelled from 'what then I was', of a personal and social education:

> For I have learned
> To look on nature, not as in the hour
> Of thoughtless youth; but hearing often-times
> The still, sad music of humanity,
> Nor harsh nor grating, though of ample power
> To chasten and subdue. And I have felt
> A presence that disturbs me with the joy
> Of elevated thoughts; a sense sublime
> Of something far more deeply interfused,
> Whose dwelling is the light of setting suns,
> And the round ocean and the living air,
> And the blue sky, and in the mind of man:
> A motion and a spirit, that impels
> All thinking things, all objects of all thought,
> And rolls through all things.

A fundamental attitude and sensibility is at work here, but I wonder if there is in that word 'learning' an echo of a choice and commitment. A verse by George Herbert springs to mind:

> A man that looks on glass,
> On it may stay his eye;
> Or if he pleaseth, through it pass,
> And then the heaven espy.

That this verse has since become a hymn may put people off. Religious vocabulary, a moralistic tone to some extent counted against 'Tintern Abbey' in that room in Edinburgh. But there was also space in that shared reading to recover what is new in this old language. As I discovered in the back of that taxi, my little childhood home could bring new meaning to the Jordan Valley.

POETRY

ELLEN STORM

Resuscitation

It comes to us all in the end, and even
after all these years, this is still my first time
to face the empty promise
that only minutes ago was a cry,
a smile and arms filled with blessings.

I am doing everything I can,
and everything right, and yet

in fresh death we float, together through fog.
I am reaching out for substance, but the mists
run through my fingertips like laughter:
the *you can't catch me* tinkling
of the playground,

and still your hands lie still – ungrasping –
and your heart is quiet.
No familiar thud in your chest;
your body slack in bloody towels
and pale as Easter snow.

White as ashes and as impossible to gather,
it drifts and flutters: becalmed.
In the distance there is shouting,
a flurry of activity and all the while
a soft, steady blowing...

a far-off four-four rhythm:
the drumbeat approaches the gate.

This book is called INTERRUPTING CHICKEN, right, Papa?
WE'RE GOING ON A
LION HUNT
"Cottrell Boyce is warm, funny and totally original." Daily Mail
THE UN-FORGOTTEN COAT
Frank Cottrell Boyce
Quentin Blake
You're Only Young Twice!

SOUTH AFRICA 2012

Niall Gibney

Niall Gibney, The Reader Organisation's Community Development Apprentice, was invited by Liverpool Football Club Foundation to accompany them on a trip to visit Whizz Kids United, a youth programme using football as a medium for HIV/Aids education in Durban, South Africa.

Liverpool to Africa. Insert one eight-hour plane journey > Get out in Dubai > Wait > Get on another eight-hour plane > Arrive at destination. I felt pretty mad as this is by far the furthest I've ever been. When we arrived we were greeted by two of the guys from Whizz Kids United and by Themba and Jongi, United Nations Apprentices and LFC ambassadors. We had a meal in our guest house, a nice little place with happy staff, and went to bed to get ready for the events starting in the morning.

We started out on the day visiting Mthethomusha Primary School – that was amazing! We walked in there and there were about 300 kids singing a traditional African song. I've never experienced anything like that and it made the hairs on my neck stand up. When the kids had finished, the LFC/Reader team gave the assembly our key messages: 'rule out the racist', 'shoot goals not guns', 'say no to knife crime', and 'you'll never walk alone'. I spoke about my experiences with knives and also talked to them about the importance of reading and education. We sang after that, dancing with no shame to big hits such as 'I Am the Music Man'!

After this we went to Edendale hospital and gave out plenty of red hats, scarves and Steven Gerrard photos to the kids on the wards where a troupe of kids with AIDS sang for us. There's no way to describe it without using clichés; it felt so unfair but they were still smiling, and strong and brave. Some home-cooked traditional African food with the Whizz Kids team was just what we needed to give us energy for a football session, so after letting the dumplings and lamb digest, we were off to coach the hospital staff team. The coaching sessions were great and you could see how those sessions would turn a man or a boy into a better footballer quite quickly.

We started the next day by visiting the Malala Primary School, the poorest school which we were able to get to on the trip. The journey to the school was a bit manic; there were all types of dogs in the road (the school was half-way up a mountain) and we were beeping at goats to move as we made our way up the muddy slopes past numerous shanty town shops and houses made of corrugated iron. Everyone who greeted us wanted to talk and take photos and there was me with all the Liverpool reps, feeling like an important guy. In truth though, the kids were happy to be visited by anyone.

It was raining so the LFC coaches had to improvise a bit and abandoned all hope of outdoor football in favour of 'indoor training' whilst I went to do some reading with some of the other kids. Their first language was Zulu, but fair play to them, they tried their best to keep up with the accent and the lingo. I know for a fact they picked up on the chicken sounds I was making during the story because they were laughing! After the reading session and the football was over, I gave out all my Reader gifts, bookmarks, pens, about fifteen copies of *A Little, Aloud for Children* and some other primary-school-age books. They were all absolutely made up; I was shocked by how happy they were to be receiving these books.

Once we had finished with the school we went for lunch with the owner and manager of a local South African Premier League team called Maritzburg United. It felt awkward to be with poor kids all morning then switch to being wined and dined on fine Indian foods and sit in the VIP box.

Our final day was only a half day (due to the evening flight home) and we visited Clarence Primary School which was clearly better off than the others in the area. The racial divide

"I had to keep telling kids I wasn't famous"

was noticeable as the kids in this school were all colours and backgrounds, especially Asian, whilst the really poor schools tended to be all black. You could also see the difference in the teachers and quality of the facilities; it would be good if all the other schools had this at their disposal. Lots of the kids came running over like we were Stevie G or something and I had to keep telling kids I wasn't famous, but they still wanted an autograph just because 'my voice was cool'. We held some training games and I read a poem with a few kids about diversity which we then performed to the rest of the guys as a present for playing such good football. After that it was time to wind down with an amazing sing song with Bill and the Whizz Kids staff and then it was off for our final meal and a bit of chilling before going home.

I had a brilliant time, I mean from the start. I suppose my vision of Africa before this trip was like a 'please give £2 a month advert' but it was completely different. I mean, yeah, you can notice the poverty and there is a lot of slum housing and shanty towns, but then you'll see half of the slum homes painted and looking much fresher and that makes you proud that no matter the people's situation they're still proud. Not only that, they're happier than we are in our supposedly developed countries. Yeah, we can go out and spend £90 on a pair of brand new Nikes and they can't, but what does that matter? Yeah, they eat cheap food every day, rice and bread for example, but it's nutritious; we've got money for food and quick availability but what do we do? Abuse it, get fat, fill our arteries up and make ourselves sluggish. If I had the choice of whether I was born in the slums of Liverpool or the slums of South Africa, I would say SA. It's a different type of poor than the struggling Englishman. We've got capitalism dangling over us constantly and you simply don't get anywhere in countries like this with no money. I was surprised by how Liverpool as a place has actually got some worse problems than Durban, gun and knife crime mainly, problems with drugs – though I know other places, like Jo'berg, are much worse in comparison to Liverpool. But Durban and the surrounding province of Kwazulu-Natal seemed all happy on the surface, although appearances can be deceptive and mostly are. I suppose if there is a heaven I would expect it to be much fuller of people from countries like this than I would countries like ours. So a big thanks to the Liverpool FC Foundation for organising and inviting me and The Reader Organisation along.

YOUR REGULARS

CALDERSTONES MANSION
INTERNATIONAL CENTRE FOR SHARED READING

Jane Davis

Talk of a 'centre' began many years ago when I registered that I was walking past a beautiful but semi-derelict building every day on my way up the hill towards the university where The Reader Organisation enjoyed some free office space. How much more could we do if we had a *building*, I thought. We would set our own tone then. And here was just such a building, neglected, unused and it had enormous potential. Soon I had a little sign that read 'The Reader Centre' pinned to my noticeboard, despite the fact that everyone I spoke to (apart from my Reader colleagues, of course) warned me sternly against the idea, especially those who had had anything to do with buildings. 'You'll spend your life worrying about the roof/boiler/tenancy agreements', people said. 'I have seen more people defeated by buildings than…'

That might be true, but I felt it differently. As a child and young person I suffered what these days is called 'being vulnerably housed' and a deep need for a secure place where one could be fully alive and *in community* with others is powerful in me. I have a home of my own which satisfies that need on a personal level, but somehow the desire for a house (etymologically from the Old English, *hus*, dwelling, shelter) doesn't simply exist on a personal level. That's why, despite the warnings, I pinned up 'The Reader Centre' sign: we didn't have an actual place yet but the thought of it was rooting in my heart. That was 2005.

That initial fantasy building was what is known in Liverpool as The Irish Centre, or the Wellington Rooms. It is still a beautiful building and still – I think – unused. Within memory it was a warm and friendly pub and meeting place.

Later, Reader staff joined me on literal excursions around and a fantasy life about the old oak-lined Education Library on the first floor of 19–26 Abercromby Square; then there was the unoccupied shop on School Lane, part of the Bluecoat; later still, I eyed some of the marked-for-closure Wirral libraries. Over and over, I was, we were, interested in something unused, neglected, at risk or unfulfilled: something that might be rehabilitated. The old themes recur and recur in a life.

Sensible people continued to remind me about costs, roofing, security. And to ask what we would do in it that we couldn't do now; what would it *add*, this dangerous, costly, creativity-sapping purpose-deflecting building?

Like a desperate child I would mutter that I knew about costs, roofing, security. I *understood* the risks! And as for what we would do there – why, we'd be happy of course! Have readings, cook good food, store our books, play. Create a quality of experience. A library, a bookshop, homemade bread, Reader's Days. Literary lunches. Grand Dinners. Gradually a Reader charity shop became part of it – somewhere we could sell our car-boot finds, polished up, our cuttings and cupcakes. And gradually it dawned on me that inside this building, there would be ways not simply to get into reading but also to get into work.

There would be jobs and whatever that activity is that comes before a job, the joining in, the feeling you may have a place in the world, the being part of something in some way that suits you. We were going to create a working community based on reading.

CALDERSTONES MANSION

© David Jones

Though many people speak of work as a necessary evil, and though I have done many grim jobs, from selling cooked meats on a market stall to serving scampi in a basket in Liverpool's 1972

"Work is the best chance most of us have for personal creativity"

She Club, for me, work is also the best chance most of us have for personal creativity; by testing our inner selves against the unwilling concrete hardness of the world we discover our powers. As a 16-year-old waitressing in a French bistro in Brighton, I discovered I had some sort of people-skill and could talk food. As a young teacher at the University of Liverpool I discovered I could share my reading and get people interested in literature. And it is not just me: in a shared reading group, a person who has not had a conversation with another human being for years may find they are a good listener, or have a persuasive tongue or sharp wit, or that they can be a peace-maker, or spot things, words, meanings others don't see. Most of us need to discover who and what we are, and what we may become, by butting up against other people, and by entering new and challenging situations as well as by sticking at things when the going is tough.

Creating jobs is for me a sort of virtuous circle which allows the benefit of creativity to spread far beyond the pleasure afforded to the artist, the entrepreneur. It is a sort of setting free of energy into the world. When making profit is part of this mix, there is usually less creative space for the working person, because the maximising of profit always takes precedence over human, or community, satisfaction. A business often exists largely to provide good returns for its investors, and most investors want cash returns. But profit might become more about service and common values, about care for our social fabric. In such a case, work would become more interesting and rewarding for more people. That is the kind of work I began to imagine in our Centre. The fantasy building became a sort of fantasy canvas on which I imagined many kinds of creative work, paid and voluntary, amateur and professional, bookish and personal. If a Get Into Reading group is a small community model, the building would be an intermediary between the shared reading group and the world. It would be our version of the world. All this and no building anywhere in sight.

But it was a couple of years ago, when I was introduced to the Peckham Centre, that my thoughts about a building began to really take off. *The Reader* featured a piece on The Peckham Centre (issue no 35). It was Rosemary Hawley, one of The Reader Organisation's trustees, and, at that time, our Chair, who introduced me to Peckham. Had I been talking about a possible building, a Reader Centre of some sort? She gave me a little pile of books, maybe three or four of them. They were all about the Peckham experiment. They didn't look terribly interesting and I do often judge a book by its cover, so I didn't read them for a while.

But then one day, I did. It was a remarkable experience, of a sort I had been lucky enough to have two or three times before, the first time, when as part of my PhD research I spent a month reading the then-uncatalogued Stapledon papers in the Special Collections of the Liverpool University Library: that was like time travel, like meeting a ghost who was still somehow alive. The powerful and growing sense, as I read, day after day, through handwritten notebooks, letters, lecture notes, of a real person fully present, with all his ideas, his thoughts, his mind, all open to me, the presence of Olaf Stapledon, author of *Last and First Men*, was deeply personal and almost overpowering. I had a similar experience when I spent months reading, very slowly, the *Collected Letters* of George Eliot, and later sill, when helping my husband with research into the Bernard Malamud collection of papers in the Harry Ransome Library at the University of Austin, Texas. Each time, this experience has been about getting a direct, immediate sense of access, unedited as it were, un-artful, with the whiff of messy reality about it, to someone's mind, another human being's powerful experience of ideas, thoughts and feelings.

Suddenly, as I read Rosemary's books, I saw that the Peckham Experiment was a very big, and still very live idea. This was an amazing experiment in wellbeing that took place between 1926 and 1950 when two doctors set up the world's first Health Centre.

It is an idea that was ahead of its time and which needs a great deal of contemporary attention. Of course there are aspects of the Peckham experiment – the emphasis on the biological family for example – which were key for them but seem almost useless to me. These I ignore. The key thing is about the creation of an opportunity for a truly open and inviting community, in which people learn of their own free will and without coercion.

Once the implications of Peckham had begun to sink it, the requirement for a building with which to complete the model which had begun with Get Into Reading (a model of community, shared reading, uncoerced and self-chosen education) became very powerful. For several years, as Director of the Reader Organisation I have been waiting for the right building opportunity to arise. It arose at Calderstones.

In January this year we heard that our year's work had come to a first stage of fruition when it was announced we had gained 'preferred bidder status' with Liverpool City Council. The project still has a long way to go, but we're off to a good start with our home city's backing for our International Centre for Reading and Wellbeing. A team of us at The Reader Organisation will now set to work with our partners Plus Dane Neighbourhood Investor, Mersey Care Mental Health Trust and the University of Liverpool's Centre for Research into Reading, Information and Linguistic Systems, to develop a social business which will support itself, and the fabric of the building into the future. We hope the Centre will open fully, after a building makeover, in 2015. In the meantime, we set off on a large scale fundraising effort and community-engagement process. We want to talk to everyone who lives locally or who uses the park, but also to everyone who feels they have a stake in developing reading.

We will develop a non-profit-distributing social business at Calderstones, which will include educational and literary courses, reading holidays, wellbeing breaks for carers and many more activities as well as providing an international HQ for The Reader Organisation.

If you would like to be kept informed of our progress please contact The Calderstones Team at The Reader Organisation.

ASK THE READER

Brian Nellist

Q I'm in a Get Into Reading group and we were reading Shakespeare's sonnet 29, 'When in disgrace with fortune' and we were expected to make some sort of sense of it without knowing, as I discovered later, that it was addressed to a male lover. Doesn't that make all the difference to its significance?

A Well it is of course good that you should be interested enough in it that you should consult critical and scholarly material but that was subsequent to your actually reading it. And I do wonder whether such information is either quite as necessary as you assume it is or quite as reliable as you think. 'Lover' today has specifically sexual implications but its use in earlier times could involve a personal warmth that was not primarily physical. The language used in some Anglo-Saxon literature to describe the relation of the vassal to his lord, his 'ring-giver', involves love, and lover is used by the devout for God Himself. In Troubadour poetry the lady is the object of veneration rather than of physical possession and Renaissance traditions of male friendship have often an intensity that is easily misinterpreted. Elizabethan sonnet sequences are written out of the strain between an admiration for the lady's beauty, purity and superiority to the lover and his desire for physical consummation. It's possible that Shakespeare the dramatist invents a plot for his sequence involving three characters, a young man who is the object of veneration, a dark lady sexually available and a lover dismayed to find the so-admired man making love to his own mistress. Think of the gender confusions in *Twelfth Night* or *As You Like It* and the argument may seem more likely. I say this not because it is a certainty but precisely because we cannot know the actual context of the poems. Scholarship uses 'facts' to create a debate, to offer persuasive argument not to establish a precise truth.

What is certain is what the literature can mean to us as we read it now, today. That love for what we read creates, of course, the desire to know more. Helen Gardner, that great editor of Donne's love poetry, tried to divide the works from his promiscuous youth from the more deeply felt poems like 'The Good Morrow' or 'The Relique' written, she argued, after his marriage. As Empson pointed out, however, he would in that case not be a very reliable husband. What is certain is what happens as you follow the arc of feeling in sonnet 29;

Yet in these thoughts myself almost despising,
Haply I think on thee...

In moments of self-doubt we may seem to be dissolved out of existence but the recognition that we are real to another person or people and even more that they are real to us restores us. More, it produces a recoil so great that we wonder whether the doubt had not happened ('Haply') precisely to produce such a recovery. The mind is not consciously playing a game with itself. Our resources of feeling live their own life, as it were, and come to our aid in unforeseen ways. Bi-polar exists as a medical term but we are all suspended perilously, if we are being honest, between extremes of doubt and faith, diffidence and certainty. As readers we find such a meaning lies beyond the debates that contextualised study exists very properly to raise.

This is not to question that a book first published in 1609 does not also carry with it a lot that has to be explained. Language changes and allusions are made to what is no longer familiar. The same is true for literature in the present. The most powerful recent novel that I've read in the past two or three years is Graham Swift's *Wish You Were Here* and when it is read in fifty or two-hundred years time then the state of the dairy industry in the late twentieth century, BSE (remember mad cows?), foot-and-mouth disease, war in Iraq and Afghanistan will all need

"Literature is that form of writing which transcends the circumstances of its birth"

explanation. But these are metaphors within which the solid truths of sibling feeling, of forms of dependence within human partnerships, of jealousies between family and sexual love, of the haunting of the mind by the memory of a particular place, that by now terrible word, 'repatriation', all that has such permanent and memorable significance in the novel, will remain available to readers. Literature is that form of writing which transcends the circumstances of its birth. Doubtless future scholars will be interested in the political contexts of the 1980s and beyond, and will discover a lot about Mr Swift's life story and survey the whole sequence of his novels. But that will not make reading the novel more certain. On the contrary, it is because it will have readers that such study will become necessary. If that were not so then books would simply become historical documents. So trust your facilitator in Get Into Reading and then, of course, if you are so interested in what you're reading that you want to find out more about it, good. But don't think that the study of its pastness takes precedence over its presentness, those significances that the group collectively but also each of us individually find full of light and depth.

BOOKS ABOUT…

AMERICAN CRIME

Angela Macmillan

It began with a visit to Boston and the decision to read something by Boston-born author Denis Lehane whom I first came across as one of the writers for the extraordinary and brilliant TV series *The Wire*. Apart from a little Chandler a long time ago, American crime fiction was unexplored territory for me and so, after some private investigation of my own, I came up with the following books, none of which disappointed.

Denis Lehane, *Mystic River* (2001)
Bantam; ISBN-13: 978-0553818246

Dave, Sean and Jimmy are playing together in the street. A car stops. It is the police who rebuke the boys for vandalism. Dave is told to get into the police car to be driven home. It is the last anyone sees of him for three days. It was not the police after all. 25 years later, Sean is a homicide detective, Jimmy an ex-con who runs a grocery store and Dave, though married, is emotionally broken. Jimmy's daughter is found murdered and the same night, Dave comes home inexplicably covered in blood. When Sean is assigned the investigation the three are brought together again. Denis Lehane is a terrific, high-energy writer who manages to be both thrilling and deeply, humanly, real.

George V. Higgins, *The Friends of Eddie Coyle* **(1972)**
Orion; ISBN-10: 1409127621

I read this short, dense crime novel (which Denis Lehane described as 'game-changing') twice over because the first time is like entering a dark room where there are only disembodied voices talking together and you have no idea who is saying what or to whom. Gradually your eyes become accustomed to the dark, you put together bits of information, begin to see where you are, what is going on. Eddie Coyle is a small-time crook in Boston, desperate to stay out of jail. The story is mostly dialogue, superbly done. You may think you have read this sort of thing before or seen it in movies, but Higgins is the Daddy.

Hillary Waugh, *Last Seen Wearing* **(1952)**
Pan Books; ISBN-13: 978-0330389891

The title appears on most of the lists of top crime novels and the book is, in a good way, a rather old fashioned police procedural story. On 3rd March 1950 a student goes missing from campus and for the next five-and-a-half weeks we follow the extraordinarily painstaking police investigation, knowing no more or less than them (except I guessed) as they straightforwardly work through the evidence. The affectionate, prickly relationship between the chief of police and his sergeant is particularly engaging.

Patricia Highsmith, *Strangers on a Train* **(1950)**
Vintage; ISBN-13: 978-0099283072

Two men; a chance meeting on a train; an agreement to murder: 'I kill your wife, you kill my mother'. Patricia Highsmith's books create an almost unbearable tension for the reader who absolutely knows that the inevitable will happen and therefore

can hardly bear to read forward but at the same time, as if hyp-
notically, can hardly bear to stop reading. Highsmith characters
never do the obvious – go to the police, tell a friend. They make
the worst possible choices, act without reason and totally out of
character. In the opening moments of this story Bruno attaches
himself to Guy's life like a human leech and from then on, there
is nothing Guy can do about it.

Ross Macdonald, *The Drowning Pool* **(1950)**
Penguin Classics; ISBN-13: 978-0141196626

Lew Archer is the tough talking, hard-boiled, likeable private eye
in Macdonald's novel in the Chandler/Hammett tradition. The
plot is pretty much what you might expect; it is the prose that
draws you into the darkness of California: 'There was nothing
wrong with Southern California that a rise in the ocean level
wouldn't cure.' Apparently, Macdonald's PhD thesis was on
Coleridge. It is wonderful to me, though not so surprising, that a
student of Coleridge can also write: 'The counterman slid a thin
white sandwich and a cup of thick brown coffee across the black
lucite bar. He had pink butterfly ears. The rest of him was still in
the larval stage'.

WHAT'S ON WATSON?
Murder in the Library: An A-Z of Crime Fiction
British Library, January 18th to May 12th 2013.

http://www.bl.uk/whatson/exhibitions/murder/index.html

A LITTLE *MORE* ALOUD

ARTHUR CONAN DOYLE
THE ADVENTURE OF THE SPECKLED BAND

Selected by Angela Macmillan

As 'Books About…' features American crime writers it is fitting that A Little More *Aloud should redress the balance with something quintessentially British. This is the eighth of the twelve stories collected in* The Adventures of Sherlock Holmes. *Holmes and Watson are sharing rooms as bachelors in Baker Street. Holmes wakes Watson early one morning to ask him to come and meet a woman who has arrived to see him in a considerable state of agitation.*

I had no keener pleasure than in following Holmes in his professional investigations, and in admiring the rapid deductions, as swift as intuitions, and yet always founded on a logical basis, with which he unravelled the problems which were submitted to him. I rapidly threw on my clothes and was ready in a few minutes to accompany my friend down to the sitting-room. A lady dressed in black and heavily veiled, who had been sitting in the window, rose as we entered.

'Good-morning, madam,' said Holmes cheerily. 'My name is Sherlock Holmes. This is my intimate friend and associate, Dr. Watson, before whom you can speak as freely as before myself.

Ha! I am glad to see that Mrs. Hudson has had the good sense to light the fire. Pray draw up to it, and I shall order you a cup of hot coffee, for I observe that you are shivering.'

'It is not cold which makes me shiver,' said the woman in a low voice, changing her seat as requested.

'What, then?'

'It is fear, Mr. Holmes. It is terror.' She raised her veil as she spoke, and we could see that she was indeed in a pitiable state of agitation, her face all drawn and grey, with restless frightened eyes, like those of some hunted animal. Her features and figure were those of a woman of thirty, but her hair was shot with premature grey, and her expression was weary and haggard. Sherlock Holmes ran her over with one of his quick, all comprehensive glances.

'You must not fear,' said he soothingly, bending forward and patting her forearm. 'We shall soon set matters right, I have no doubt. You have come in by train this morning, I see.'

'You know me, then?'

'No, but I observe the second half of a return ticket in the palm of your left glove. You must have started early, and yet you had a good drive in a dog-cart, along heavy roads, before you reached the station.'

The lady gave a violent start and stared in bewilderment at my companion.

'There is no mystery, my dear madam,' said he, smiling. 'The left arm of your jacket is spattered with mud in no less than seven places. The marks are perfectly fresh. There is no vehicle save a dog-cart which throws up mud in that way, and then only when you sit on the left-hand side of the driver.'

'Whatever your reasons may be, you are perfectly correct,' said she. 'I started from home before six, reached Leatherhead at twenty past, and came in by the first train to Waterloo. Sir, I can stand this strain no longer; I shall go mad if it continues. I have no one to turn to – none, save only one, who cares for me, and he, poor fellow, can be of little aid. I have heard of you, Mr. Holmes; I have heard of you from Mrs. Farintosh, whom you helped in the hour of her sore need. It was from her that I had your address. Oh, sir, do you not think that you could help me, too, and at least throw a little light through the dense darkness which surrounds me? At present it is out of my power to reward you for your services, but in a month or six weeks I shall be married, with the control of my own income, and then at least you shall not find me ungrateful.'

Holmes turned to his desk and, unlocking it, drew out a small case-book, which he consulted.

'Farintosh,' said he. 'Ah yes, I recall the case; it was concerned with an opal tiara. I think it was before your time, Watson. I can only say, madam, that I shall be happy to devote the same care to your case as I did to that of your friend. As to reward, my profession is its own reward; but you are at liberty to defray whatever expenses I may be put to, at the time which suits you best. And now I beg that you will lay before us everything that may help us in forming an opinion upon the matter.'

'Alas!' replied our visitor, 'the very horror of my situation lies in the fact that my fears are so vague, and my suspicions depend so entirely upon small points, which might seem trivial to another, that even he to whom of all others I have a right to look for help and advice looks upon all that I tell him about it as the fancies of a nervous woman. He does not say so, but I can read it from his soothing answers and averted eyes. But I have heard, Mr. Holmes, that you can see deeply into the manifold wickedness of the human heart. You may advise me how to walk amid the dangers which encompass me.'

'I am all attention, madam.'

READERS CONNECT
VINTAGE CLASSICS

ERNEST HEMINGWAY
THE SNOWS OF KILIMANJARO

A disparate group of these stories from early in Hemingway's career focuses on the partly autobiographical character Nick Adams in his boyhood, through First-World War experiences,

and on his life as a young man in Europe and at home in Michigan. But you don't become familiar with Nick. Hemingway's pared-down language is directive rather than descriptive or literary – it gives commands to attention – and while this style can be both refreshing and head-clearing, it also means that the stories stay remote and difficult, just as strangers do.

Intimacy is awkward, as in 'Up in Michigan' where Liz's romantic fantasy about Jim leads to a rough out-of-doors seduction. Afterwards, crying, she wraps her coat around the sleeping man and walks home alone. Wanting reassurance, she instead gives comfort to the man who is too drunk to be shaken awake. Will her coat mean something to him when he stirs? Is her action wasted? Those *unasked* questions are the measure of the closeness Hemingway's prose allows.

His special talent in these stories is to show how thought or action changes things fleetingly. In 'The Three-Day Blow', Nick and his friend talk of Nick's lucky escape from a relationship that had become claustrophobic but as they talk Marge secretly becomes to Nick 'all that mattered'. His friend resolves never to talk of it again, warning 'You might get back into it again'. Nick replies: ' "There's always that danger." He felt happy now. There was not anything that was not irrevocable.' Within a half-page, this transformation too is overthrown.

Lynne Hatwell (dovegreyreader) is a Devon-based community nurse

I couldn't get into Hemingway at all, which I think may say more about me than him at the moment as I have enjoyed his short stories in the past. I could see all the things I have liked in him but did not feel them. I wonder if his deliberately flat style means you have to be in the mood for him more than with other writers.
* *

Mette Steenberg is the founder/director of Laeseforeningen (The Reading Society) in Denmark

This man writes arrestingly well and opens the details of the perceptible world for your eyes. Contrary to my prejudgment his interest reaches beyond fishing. I liked best the stories in which human (inter)actions are displayed in their psychological nudity – although the same nudity gives me a feeling of something missing, at times horrendously missing as in 'On the Quai at Smyrna'.
* * * *

Drummond Moir, once of Edinburgh, works for a London-based publisher

I find it very, very difficult to like Hemingway. His famously stark, sparse prose can be very powerful given the frequently horrifying subject matter, but it can also feel bald, flat and (sorry!) quite unrelentingly dull. I found 'The Soldier's Home' was very poignant, but I'd struggle to recommend the rest of this collection.
*

STAR RATINGS

***** one of the best books I've read
**** one of the best I've read this year
*** highly recommended

** worth reading
* not for me but worth trying
0 don't bother

BUCK'S QUIZ

NAME THAT SLEUTH

Angela Macmillan

1. 'In height he was rather over six feet, and so excessively lean that he seemed to be considerably taller. His eyes were sharp and piercing, save during those intervals of torpor to which I have alluded; and his thin, hawk-like nose gave his whole expression an air of alertness and decision.'

2. He was hardly more than five feet four inches but carried himself with great dignity. His head was exactly the shape of an egg, and he always perched it a little on one side. His moustache was very stiff and military.

3. Slightly over six feet and weighs about 190 pounds. He first lived at the Hobart Arms, on Franklin Avenue near North Kenmore Avenue but then moved to the Bristol Hotel where he stayed for about ten years. His office telephone number is Glenview 7537. He generally refuses to take divorce cases.

4. A short little man with a moon face and blinking, owlish eyes, who wears a black cassock and a clerical shovel hat, and carries a large, shabby black umbrella.

5. Born in 1947 and grew up in a prefab, the son of a stage hypnotist. Suffered a nervous breakdown after leaving the SAS.

6. 'His jaw was long and bony, his chin a jutting V under the more flexible V of his mouth. His nostrils curved back to make another, smaller, V. His yellow-grey eyes were horizontal. The V motif was picked up again by thickish brows rising outward from twin creases above a hooked nose, and his pale brown hair grew down – from high flat temples – in a point on his forehead. He looked rather pleasantly like a blond Satan.'

7. She lives in River Heights, has a housekeeper named Hannah, her dad, Carson, is a lawyer. She has reddish blonde hair. Her best friends, George (Georgia) and Bess (Elizabeth) are cousins.

8. Average height, with straw-coloured hair, a beaked nose, and a vaguely foolish face. He also possessed considerable intelligence and athletic ability, evidenced by his playing cricket for Oxford University while earning a First. At aged 40 he was able to turn three cartwheels in the office corridor and he wears a monocle.

9. He is a great fan of the opera. While in his car he regularly listens to recordings of famous opera singers such as Maria Callas. He has few close friends, an unhealthy lifestyle and is diagnosed with diabetes.

10. Born around 1884, he is stocky and of average height. This man is a pipe smoker who likes to visit bars and cafés during investigations, for a meal, a beer or white wine. He usually wears a heavy overcoat.

Cassandra   No.41

ACROSS

* **1 & 17 down.** Early writer in residence at the Post Office? (7, 8)
* **5.** Bishop's chaplain and Job's friend in 11, poles apart is implied (7)
9. Certain witch hunts can reveal an early form of conscience (5)
* **10.** Optional office for the cathedral precentor, held by 28 (3, 6)
* **11 & 2 down.** Webster turned carthorse loose in the diocese (10, 6)
12. To begin with some chefs use mustard to form a layer on top (4)
14. Not native by chance (12)
18. Skin loss caused by random rabies (12)
21. Fleece extract (4)
22. Fragile young ladies as likely to come from Dresden as Beijing (5, 5)
25. This style of suit needs a pair (3, 6)
26. Weltschmerz in Paris perhaps (5)
27. Smelling stronger, must be old Edinburgh, right? (7)
* **28.** Holder of 10's office for ten years (7)

*Clues with an asterisk have a common theme

DOWN

1. In taking arms against Irak I'm bound to adopt this stance (6)
* **2.** See 11 across
3. Deceitful quartet may present themselves in this guise (10)
4. Recollected strange creatures in the site yard (5)
5. Proverbially these can't be made without breakages (9)
6. Outpouring of grief in a last goodbye (4)
7. Electrical component he installs in office (8)
8. Furthest back fall prey to the devil (8)
13. Greets new born excitedly with potent drink (6, 4)
15. Treat rash created by woodland fungus (9)
16. Can measure distance from Toronto Dome terrestrial telescope (8)
* **17.** See 1 across
19. Leaders of Buddhist regime under north east Indian member of the Commonwealth (6)
20. Putting question in the role of monarch (6)
23. Choral comes in just under double figures (5)
24. Unleavened bread in puritan rite (4)

PRIZES

The winner of the Crossword (plucked in time-honoured tradition from a hat) will receive a book prize courtesy of Vintage Classics, and the same to the winner of the fiendishly difficult Buck's Quiz.

Congratulations to Steve Bowkett of Cardiff and Tony Anstey of Birkenhead (Buck's Quiz), Pam Nixon from Oxford and Steve Bowkett (Crossword).

Please send your solutions (marked Cassandra Crossword or Buck's Quiz) to The Reader Organisation, The Friary Centre, Bute Street, Liverpool, L5 3LA. The deadline for answers is 10 April, 2013.

ANSWERS

CASSANDRA CROSSWORD NO. 40

Across
1. Ossify **4.** Easter **9.** Stye **10.** Discipline **11.** Bitter **12.** Excepted **13.** Shapelier **15.** Boss **16.** Hair **17.** Strategic **21.** Oratorio **22.** Denial **24.** Redemption **25.** Dais **26.** Tastes **27.** George

Down
1. Ostrich **2.** Sweet **3.** Federal **5.** Apiece **6.** Telephone **7.** Ringers **8.** Isoelectronic **14.** Pointless **16.** Herbert **18.** Andante **19.** Imagine **20.** Triple **23.** Nadir

BUCK'S QUIZ NO. 47

1. Humbert Humbert (*Lolita*) **2.** Seamus Heaney **3.** *Tristram Shandy* **4.** In a barley field near Florence **5.** *Changing Places,* David Lodge **6.** John Donne **7.** Craig Raine **8.** Jimmy and Alison Porter (*Look Back in Anger*) **9.** Melvyn Bragg (*A Time to Dance*) **10.** *The Crimson Petal and the White* **11.** Gloire de Dijon Roses, D.H.Lawrence **12**. *The Perfumed Garden*

MALCOLM BENNETT AND FRIEND
BUTLINS, 1965

ESSAY

BEST FRIENDS

Malcolm Bennett

'm writing this while sitting on the sofa at my dad's house. He's not very well so I've come to stay for a few days not least to make sure he eats properly. He's decided he's had enough – its half past seven – so he's off to bed. Snuggled up against me is his dog, a westie who, because I'm a useless son who rarely visits, I've never met before. But we're already good friends. We've been for a walk, I've fed her twice and we've played with her cloth toy. And now she's decided that that's enough for her too, so she's gone through to dad's bedroom and is lying down near his feet – a kind of combination foot-rest-hot-water-bottle.

There are sixteen million dogs and cats in the UK, and according to the Pet Food Manufacturers Association (who, incidentally, banned the use of bovine offal in pet foods for fear of BSE some time before the government banned it from human foods), around a half of British households have a pet of some kind. That's not counting fish, which I suppose are really more home decor than pets anyway. These non-fishy pets are very much seen as members of the family. In one PFMA survey a few years ago, not only did 60% of single people say they kept a pet for companionship but 39% of them claimed to have 'replaced' their (presumably ex-) partner with one. Yet how many households in your favourite TV or radio soap/drama have a pet? And other than Snowy and whatever that dog in the Famous Five was

"An aspirational chihuahua might be likely to end up as lunch if he tried it on with a wolf"

called, the one in the night time and the other one that didn't bark, how many dogs appear in any literature (don't cheat by googling it). So much for gritty realism.

Biologically speaking, all dogs are, of course, fundamentally the same, not only as each other but as their wild ancestors the wolves, with whom they can to this day still readily interbreed. Well, maybe not readily. An aspirational chihuahua might be more likely to end up as lunch than a proud father if he tried it on with a wolf. For that matter, he would need not only courage but a step ladder to get very far with most other domestic dogs. But my point is that, fundamentally, all dogs are, for all their outward diversity, very similar. Even the variation that we see in dogs is missing in cats, however. Although the human relationship with cats goes back a long way – some 9,500 years – cats still walk alone and it could be argued that they have adopted and perhaps domesticated us rather than the other way around. I'm sure that's how they think of it. Our relationship with dogs goes back much further though. There are even suggestions that early 'modern' *Homo sapiens* and dogs working together may have contributed to our managing to out-compete our Neanderthal neighbours.

There's recently been a TV series that followed some of the work done by my colleagues in the Veterinary School. I'm not in it: some might say this is because not everyone yet has a wide-screen TV, others that too many have HD. Whatever, my contributions were limited to trying to keep crew and colleagues on speaking terms, supplying occasional 'factoids' and checking voice-over scripts. My reason for mentioning this is that while

I learned a lot from my involvement about how TV is made, it reminded me that I am in that 50% who have pets and therefore have daily contact with (non-human) animals, and that life and attitudes can be different for the other 50%. Perhaps it's this other 50% who write? The interest for many of the crew was not in the animals or their ailments but the emotional energy the owners put into those animals and their health - the animals were largely there to provide a framework for human stories. I guess this is also why almost all of the stories, including most of the 'farm' animal stories, concerned pets, including pet pigs, pet goats and alpacas, rather than animals-we-keep-to-eat.

I'm finishing writing this on the train home from my dad's. He's looking better though nothing like best. As well as his dog he's got fantastic neighbours – well, friends really – some of whom I remember calling uncle or aunty as a child so I find it difficult to call them by just their first names now, others I went to school with, and a few new-comers who only moved in around twenty years ago. When I was a small boy (40-plus years ago) it was a country lane with cows in the field at the bottom of the garden and a mile or more walk to the nearest bus stop: now the buses roar down the lane and the field is a housing estate where the streets are named Swinburne, Orwell, Auden and Keats. And the farm at the bottom of the lane, near the mill stream, where they used to keep pigs outside in muddy sties is now an alternative therapy centre for London commuters. My dad's dog is somebody to moan at, chatter to, complain about, celebrate with, care for and look after, and you don't have to be overly anthropomorphic to know she gives the same back. The neighbours take her for walks and bring her treats. When I walk her, people know who I am because I'm with her: ' 'Ow's yer dad?' they ask. She is an important and integral part of that community and my passport to my old home.

FICTION

SWAN

Greg Forshaw

Autumn, twilight, and Lauren works on after the stylists have gone, stripping the salon of that day's growth of hair.

Already she's brought a solar shine from the sinks and tiles to match that of the mirrors.

She's still to stock up and lay out, hoover and mop. Not to forget that last fix for everything loose – chairs, tables, glossies – prior to the area manager's arrival tomorrow.

The late working is not unlike the clubbing she's going to do after it, Lauren can get lost in either, and so isn't surprised when she finds herself at the front window, again. The hot lighting lowered, the salon reduced to the street's now fully fallen darkness, Lauren watching without being watched – watching for what is less clear.

Untroubled by the cobbles or the humpback bridge, cars fly by. There are few pedestrians this crisp night, excepting the one hunched figure just across the way. No, this person has paused to bend over the bridge, search the slow grey river below. Nothing. Lauren highers the lighting once more, bleaching every shadow. Nothing, really.

Banshees at the front window scare her silly.

'Oh!'

Lauren jumps and turns to see the girls dolled up, clacking

their boutique-bought nails against the glass and shaking their hair extensions at her. Already in high spirits and only halfway to town.

She crosses the salon to shriek back but the girls are gone. Lauren smiles, her eyes flicking across the way to a figure folded in shadow and somehow hovering.

No, the shape is up on the bridge's edge. Is it the person from earlier? Ages ago. Lauren knows this is not nothing – is someone about to jump. Knows because the stilled air attends it, and the air alone. There's no one else about.

Lauren turns away and returns to work. She knows she mustn't fall – mustn't, she means, get sidetracked. It's not her business. Getting finished is. Happily, little needs doing to the trio of leather chairs, their panels shone by the succession of women who've topped up their hope here.

She considers the girls. Her old friends are probably talking about old times, talk that never strayed beyond those years when they were girls, still at school, their lives not heavily in their own hands. No, no, they're probably already past that prelude to the usual piss and puke across this town they know too well.

'Oh, for God's sake!'

Because Lauren's really having to concentrate on the polishing and even then the hand with the cloth keeps planing off the panels.

Surely someone will come? A friend, a police officer, a random. Anyone else. Lauren lowers the lighting and returns to the window but doesn't look out. Instead she stares back at the Vax and the clippings she's piled beside it to hoover later, every hair irreversible.

Whether Lauren watches or not, however, a life may end. From the bridge there's a thirty-foot drop. She's seen. So with her face now to the freezing window, and her breath pushing at the glass, and the night pressing back, Lauren looks and looks.

Outside, a prowling GTI crests the hump then idles on spying the shadow – like it, seeming to hover – before screeching off the bridge, only to do a U-ey and come slinking back to purr,

'Jump – Jump – Jump –'

Lauren can't stand to watch *this*. She highers the lighting, opens the door, and steps into the shaft of sun thrown from the salon. Struck, the GTI bolts, a spoor of scorched rubber rising off the road. The figure steps down from the shadows and follows the light to Lauren.

Oh.

In a duffel coat with the hood up, though it hasn't been raining, the person is a woman, and old – forty easy. She halts on the threshold and breathes the salon's brassy air.

'Bunch of animals in this town,' Lauren says.

'The world's a hateful place.'

'The –? It was just boys being boys,' Lauren counters, frowning, after showing the woman inside and round to the middle chair.

'This is nice, though, your place.'

Oblivious to the deposits she's left on Lauren's floor – not mopped yet, not the point. Mud! And from where?

'You're wrong, the salon isn't mine.'

'You're keen.'

'Keen to finish.' Lauren knows you aren't meant to like work too much. 'I don't do this often.'

'Me neither.'

'Sorry?'

But the woman is shrugging off her coat, staring at herself if not Lauren in the facing mirror. She fingers her hood-smothered hair, colourless and long.

'Could you cut it?' she asks.

'I'm sorry, I can't. I'm not qualified as a stylist. I'd make a mess.'

'More of a mess you mean.'

She nearly smiles but Lauren laughs, and moves closer; the woman's eyes are the blue of fresh bruises.

'I could clean it,' Lauren says. 'As well as salons, I do hair.'

Or she's seen how it's done.

In response the woman only closes her eyes. Lauren refills the sink and attaches the shower to the faucet. She reverses the chair, wraps a towel around the woman's neck, and lowers her towards the steaming basin.

Lauren wonders if this can be work, because she likes it also:

to touch, to alter. The woman's hair softens, the water clouds over, the weight of dirt lifts.

Highering the chair again, Lauren combs out the auburn hair, cutting the clumps into clean, gleaming rows.

'That was good of you,' the woman says, her eyes opening to finally find Lauren's in the misted mirror. Blinking, she stands unsteadily. 'Still, I should let you get on.'

'Okay,' Lauren says, then winces. 'You certainly shouldn't do that.'

'What?'

'Towel dry.'

'Why?' But she stops rubbing her head and knots the towel up in her hair.

'Towel drying is wrong. It ruins your roots.'

'I could do without mine,' the woman smiles tightly, and perches on the edge of the chair. 'As I said – did I say? – I've never had my hair done in a salon before.'

'Really?'

'Mother,' the woman shrugs.

'You're close?'

'Claustrophobic.'

Oh.

'You wouldn't understand.'

Which is why stylists stick to chitchat about slebs and boyfriends and coming summer holidays. But actually Lauren's mum doesn't like salons either, and could only trust herself to cut her daughter's hair, leaving it long enough to weave, a flaxen plait of years that fell to the small of the back. To mark her seventeenth birthday Lauren got the lot cut off, and got this job as a junior to boot. The girls didn't know her that celebratory night, though her mum had no such trouble. 'Like that, is it?' was all she said. More than wilful, however, Lauren felt lighter and oddly readied – for what was less clear.

'No,' the woman continues, 'how could you understand? You're so young.'

This is the oldest I've ever been, Lauren doesn't say, her very thought on first entering the salon six months earlier. In the clearing mirror she eyes herself, metamorphosed, made adult, still sporting the pixie cut she'd found herself to suit. Adulthood wasn't as simple as a haircut, of course, and yet – But Lauren says,

'I understand that they have us at heart, our mums.'

'Until that organ gives out and leaves us where? All Mother did for me was everything, not just my hair. And when she fell ill she couldn't even do for herself, which is what killed her, never the MS. Of course Mother considered suicide: pills not a bridge. Always there before me, I shouldn't laugh.'

If that's what that drowned sound was.

'Better laughter than a bridge,' Lauren says. 'Is your mum why?'

'I don't know why. I'm borderline something. You're right, though, there should be a good reason.'

'Maybe that's what you were looking for?'

'Sorry?'

'On the bridge,' Lauren says, 'it seemed like you were searching for something, a reason?'

'No! A swan.'

'A –?'

'Swan.'

'In this town?'

'Yes, I was thinking how lovely one would be, white as a ghost but somehow more solid than anything else, and not sinking. The swan would pass under the bridge and back over the border and to see this I'd get down, and easily.'

'Maybe next time,' Lauren says, then winces.

'I hope there won't be one, because this time there was you.'

She slips her coat back on and Lauren shows her to the door, where the woman fails to fumble the latch open.

'Here, let me.'

While Lauren obliges, the woman buttons her coat against the rush of cold then hovers once more, as though waiting for a guiding word, as though Lauren has one, apart from towel. The woman looks to the street then the salon, her eyes widening.

At what? The mess she's left behind?

'Your hoover!' the woman says. 'Can you see? The squat body, the bowed neck, the way it would glide across the tiles – no?'

'Not really.'

But the woman's beside herself, bringing her hands to her head. 'Oops!' She unties the towel and her straggly locks fall free.

'Don't forget that cut,' Lauren says.

When the woman leaves, her hair is still damp and steams as she walks away – as she crosses the bridge like it isn't there. Which it is.

There's no point meeting the girls in town now – she might be joining them over the bridge home at this rate. Nevertheless Lauren's sluiced the warm suds down the basin. She's stocked up the shelves in branded rainbows and laid out the clips and combs, scissors and styling equipment, as a theatre nurse would scalpels and such before surgery. Lauren could do that, if she never graduates to styling. No need for chitchat! She's mopped the muddied floor and saved till last the hoovering, her very favourite.

The piled curls of cut hair whirl, all colours and kinks mingling before disappearing without trace. Or not quite. Much as she loves using it, Lauren hates emptying the hoover. Hates it for the same reason she keeps her own hair short, as she explained when the woman queried this on the verge of the night.

'Look, I totally trust the stylists. It's just that –'

'What?'

Lauren eyed the bridge over the woman's shoulder.

'Hair's dead, isn't it?'

'That's cheery!'

'No,' Lauren said, 'that it doesn't look lifeless on your head is thanks to places like this, to keeping on coming to them.'

Hair does look dead in the cylinder, mind. The grey grey end of everything, beyond even the alchemy of the salon. Much as she hates it, however, Lauren can empty the hoover. Doesn't have to see it as a swan either – though that *would* make this the scruff of its neck she has hold of. A swan! Maybe the woman wasn't wrong about *everything*.

CONTRIBUTORS

Ourit Ben-Haim is a street photographer based in NYC. 'The moment itself is an independent story. No matter where I take the photo, my focus is always, simply, on the moment and on the individual'.

Malcom Bennett keeps chickens and bees, and is frequently an embarrassment to his family. By way of a job, he studies zoonoses, the diseases that human animals get from non-human animals.

John Burnside's new collection of short stories, *Something Like Happy,* was published in January 2013. Among other things, he teaches a Literature and Ecology course at St Andrews and has an occasional column on nature in *The New Statesman.*

Veronika Carnaby, is an American author who has garnered international recognition for her Beat-style prose. Her pieces have appeared in such publications and functions as The Ed Sullivan Show blog, *SESAC Magazine,* SXSW, the SESAC New York Music Awards, and *Dan's Papers Literary Journal.* Her debut novel, *Bohemia,* was published in 2012.

David Constantine's most recent story collection is *Tea at the Midland* (Comma 2012). His latest poetry collection *Nine Fathoms Deep* is published by Bloodaxe. With his wife Helen he edits *Modern Poetry in Translation.*

Greg Forshaw lives in York and works for the NHS. A short he co-wrote for the UK Film Council, *uncle fran,* was shown at the 2011 London Short Film Festival. His story *The Handyman* appeared in the Fall 2012 issue of *Eclectica* (www.eclectica.org).

Niall Gibney is Community Development Assistant at The Reader Organisation.

Jackie Kay is an award-winning writer of poetry, fiction and plays. Born and brought up in Scotland, she has published five collections of poetry for adults and several for children. She was awarded an MBE in 2006. Her most recent collection of short stories is *Reality, Reality* (Picador 2012).

John Kinsella's most recent book is *Activist Poetics: Anarchy in the Avon Valley* (Liverpool University Press, 2010). His latest poetry volume is, *Armour,* (Picador) November 2011. He is a Fellow of Churchill College, Cambridge, and a Professorial Research Fellow at University of Western Australia.

Matthew Howard lives in Norwich where he works for the RSPB. He is also working on a PhD that considers the poetry of birds. Previous poems have appeared in magazines including *The Rialto, Magma, The North* and *Poetry Salzburg Review.*

Ian McMillan was born in 1956 and has been a freelance writer/performer /broadcaster since 1981. He presents *The Verb* on BBC Radio 3 every Friday night.

Michael O'Neill's two collections of poems are *The Stripped Bed* (Collins Harvill, 1990) and *Wheel* (Arc, 2008). He is the co-author (with Michael D. Hurley) of *Poetic Form: An Introduction* (CUP, 2012).

Ellen Storm has been writing poems for about nine years. She is training to be a children's doctor in the Mersey region and is the mother of two-year-old twin girls. Apart from poetry she enjoys vegan cooking and getting outdoors.

Dennis Walder is Emeritus Professor of Literature at the Open University. He has published short stories, and numerous critical books and articles on 19th and 20th century literature, including *Dickens and Religion*, *Literature in the Modern World* and, most recently, *Postcolonial Nostalgias*.

Distribution Information

Trade orders Contact Mark Chilver, Magazine Department, Central Books

> email: mark@centralbooks.com
> web: www.centralbooks.com
> tel: 0845 458 9925   fax: 0845 458 9912
> Central Books, 99 Wallis Road, London, E9 5LN

All other queries regarding trade orders or institutional subscriptions
Contact The Reader Office

> email: magazine@thereader.org.uk
> tel: 0151 207 7207

SUBSCRIBE

the reader